# POWERFUL BOOK
# INTRODUCTIONS

# POWERFUL BOOK INTRODUCTIONS

## LEADING WITH MEANING FOR DEEPER THINKING

KATHLEEN FAY, CHRISIE MORITZ,
AND SUZANNE WHALEY

Foreword by Pat Johnson

Stenhouse
PUBLISHERS

Portland, Maine

Stenhouse Publishers
www.stenhouse.com

*Credits*
Original cover photo: Suzanne Whaley
Cover design, interior design, and typesetting: Alessandra S. Turati


Library of Congress Cataloging-in-Publication Data

Names: Fay, Kathleen, 1967- author. | Moritz, Chrisie, 1977- author. |
  Whaley, Suzanne, 1966- author.
Title: Powerful book introductions : leading with meaning for deeper thinking
  / Kathleen Fay, Chrisie Moritz, and Suzanne Whaley.
Description: Portland, Maine : Stenhouse Publishers, [2017] | Includes
  bibliographical references and index.
Identifiers: LCCN 2017010327 (print) | LCCN 2017026893 (ebook) | ISBN
  9781625310514 (ebook) | ISBN 9781625310507 (pbk. : alk. paper)
Subjects: LCSH: Guided reading.
Classification: LCC LB1050.377 (ebook) | LCC LB1050.377 .F39 2017 (print) |
  DDC 372.41/62--dc23
LC record available at https://lccn.loc.gov/2017010327


Manufactured in the United States of America

 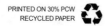

*For Sigrid Ryberg and Carol Franz,*

*courageous leaders who have always celebrated the*

*thinking teacher*

# CONTENTS

# FOREWORD

I often lend my professional books to colleagues, but I do so with a warning: "Sorry, but I really mark up my books with underlined passages, highlighting, comments in the margins, and dozens of notes on the end pages. Hope this doesn't distract from your reading." When they return a book, they tell me they got a chuckle out of my notes like "Hmm" or "YES!!!" or "What would Allington think about that?"

I value the conversations we have as these teachers finish the books. Each one of them is a true learner. And the three authors of this text are definitely in that category. Kathleen Fay, Chrisie Moritz, and Suzanne Whaley attend conferences, explore research questions, collaborate with others, and spend the necessary time thinking and reflecting on their craft. I was thrilled to hear that they would join together to write on the critical topic of supporting readers with meaning-making through book introductions, and I was eager to mark up the pages of the text they sent me with new ahas, ideas, and wonderings they evoked.

Teachers have valid questions about book introductions, like "Am I doing too much?" "Is this enough support?" "Should I mention the tricky words?" and "How much do I let the kids talk?" In *Powerful Book Introductions*, authors Kath, Chrisie, and Suzanne address these questions by sharing their planning processes so that teachers are empowered to decide what makes most sense for their students who are embarking on reading a text for the first time.

The writing in this book is not only clear and concise, but also filled with compassion and humility. Through an ongoing conversation with you, their readers, Kath, Chrisie, and Suzanne continually return to what Marie Clay always has said: "If this child is not learning to read, then I haven't figured out how to teach him yet." No matter what level of experience you have with book introductions, your knowledge will spiral upward as you read this text.

When I work with teachers, I often talk about active participation. How can we get kids to self-initiate problem solving? Are we sending the right messages to our students so that they realize their job is to make meaning of the text? What I love about this book is that the authors weave the thread of actively making meaning through every aspect of the guided reading lesson, from analyzing texts to find a good match for a certain group to planning a thoughtful book introduction to the discussion phase after the students have read the book on their own. As the authors say in this book's first chapter: "Powerful introductions serve as doorways, leading students down the path of actively constructing meaning. Effective book introductions ground readers' thinking and teach them how to use meaning to develop a rich understanding on their own."

After all, isn't that what reading is all about? Getting students to comprehend, understand, make the content their own, synthesize the information, and read at a deeper level? According to Kath, Chrisie, and Suzanne, there is no question about it: we must "lead with meaning." Kids need to "search for meaning and relevance in what they read."

I was especially intrigued when I read Chapter 3 on meaning and launching statements. Many of us, myself included, have led a book introduction and then sent students off with a reminder of the skill or strategy we have been working on—"Remember to notice those quotation marks" or "Remember if a word starts with *ch-* to get your mouth ready for that beginning sound" or "When you are stuck on a word, remember to think about what would make sense, sound right, and look right." Yet, if we believe that the students' primary task is to make meaning of the text, we should be leading with meaning by making sure that we send them off to read with the ideas of the text in mind. I think you'll also find this chapter to be very rewarding.

I'm always in awe of watching comedians do improvisation. The funny stuff they say and do comes quickly and naturally. When you see a teacher doing a good introduction, it's similar. You wonder, "How did she do that?" The answer lies in the thinking that came prior to the lesson. When I watch teachers doing a book introduction well, here's what I notice. They

- seem to know the strengths, weaknesses, and interests of the kids in the group;

- know the gist of story and what it's really about beyond the literal level;

- don't do all the talking;

- don't go page by page;

- keep it short;

- bring kids' attention to something important, whether it's the structure of the text or some confusing language structure or vocabulary; and

- send students off to read with a focus on meaning.

In this book, the authors slow down that thinking process for you, so you can see the thoughtful planning they put into their book introductions. Certainly, paying attention to multiple aspects of the text (the sentence structure, the gist of the story, the vocabulary, the new things the child will encounter, and on and on) takes time. And even though book introductions are a small part of what we do to support readers, giving careful attention to their planning sets students up to think deeply right from the start. As you read this book, you too will develop the habits of mind necessary for this level of planning, and in doing so, providing supportive book introductions will become second nature to you.

To that end, you will not find scripted lessons to follow verbatim in *Powerful Book Introductions* because these authors know that scripted lessons ignore the varied needs of the children in front of you. Nor do they suggest that you "just preteach the tricky words," because they know that may inadvertently lead readers to focus at the word level. Instead, they include actual scenarios along with stories from their own experiences and classrooms as well as analogies that make the information easy to understand. They encourage you to think and reflect. Take their ideas and practice them in your own classrooms. When you are finished with this book, you will "trust in the decisions you make as a teacher."

So, I invite you to read this book reflectively with pen or highlighter in hand. Mark up the margins with "Try this!" "Need to think about!" "Hmm" or other reflections that come to mind. Share it with friends and colleagues and let it spark professional conversations about your work. I believe the knowledge you gain from *Powerful Book Introductions* will help you support your readers more effectively than you ever imagined.

Have fun learning!

—Pat Johnson

# ACKNOWLEDGMENTS

We are fortunate to work in Fairfax County Public Schools, a school system that values adult learning as much as the learning of children. The ideas in this book come from years of learning alongside inspiring leaders and colleagues, and we owe a debt of gratitude to many.

Thank you to Jen Baskette-Tierney, Suzanne Fisher, and Michelle Holtzclaw, whose teaching is shared in this book. We wish the transcripts could capture the faces of your students, eager to read after your introductions. Many teachers sent us audio recordings of book introductions or invited us to watch them teach so that we could think together about how introductions affect the way kids understand text: Carrie Cantillana, Catherine Giacomo, Rachel Gottheim, Jodi Maher, Lauren Schrum, Julie Steinberg, Christy Thompson, Ashley Tingler, Tricia Tyskowski, Courtney Varner, and Kelly Zeigler. Their students are indeed lucky to work with them daily.

We especially want to recognize the teachers and administrators with whom we spent many hours coaching at Bailey's Elementary, London Towne Elementary, and Annandale Terrace Elementary. Teaching in front of your peers can feel risky, but these colleagues were up for the challenge of working together to figure out ways to better teach our kids. We all learned a lot during each session. An additional thanks to our fellow coaches with whom we shared many hours considering what books might really be about: Laura Bailey, Shele Banford, Jen Baskette-Tierney, Renee Brown, Debbie Demers, Mary Domes, Lindsay Duch, Lisa Felder, Jen Ganci, Hillary Garrett, Charlotte Gonzalez, Amy Greene, Lisa Holm, Sara Kugler, Kim Morrison, Charlene O'Brien, Judith Valdivielso, and Catherine Weiss. Thank you as well to

Erin Blake, Karen Cathey, Linda Randall, and Jacqui Alfriend for the many conversations about powerful instruction for beginning readers.

We have been fortunate to be part of Reading Recovery and Literacy Collaborative professional development models. Both are built on empowering teachers to understand the rationales of the complex decisions we make while teaching children. We would like to thank Cindy Downend, Irene Fountas, Kathy Harrell, Tina Henry, Andrea McCarrier, Gay Pinnell, Diane Powell, Sigrid Ryberg, Helen Sisk, and Jananne Waller for helping us consider the child's perspective and for encouraging our questions so that we are continually improving as a profession.

Philippa Stratton encouraged us to write again and helped us whittle our ideas down to book introductions. Terry Thompson, our developmental editor, was exactly who we needed to finally get us into gear and write this book. From his first reply to the outline, we breathed a collective sigh of relief and thought, "He gets us." Throughout this process, every one of the phone calls, emails, and texts kept us energized, positive, and moving forward. And most importantly, his thoughtful feedback on our drafts helped us consider the readers' perspectives. Thanks, "Charlie"! Pat Johnson, our longtime mentor, read the entire book in various stages. Her nudges, questions, and words of encouragement were invaluable. In the early days of this book, Lauren Nye Schrum paved the path of this work with Kath. We are grateful for her friendship, wisdom, and insightful teaching. Sara Kugler, Amy Greene, Mary Anne Buckley, Lindsay Duch, Lee Morales, Tess Pardini, and Nora Brent provided feedback and encouragement to keep writing. The Stenhouse team, especially Tori Bachman and Chandra Lowe, was very patient and offered encouragement from afar. We are honored to work with such professionals.

To our families: Ben and Rachel Merrifield; Austin and Aubrey Adams; Dan, Willie, and Charlotte Henry. This has been a long process and we are grateful for your patience and encouragement. Rachel, Willie, Charlotte, and Aubrey remind us daily how important and delightful it is to lead with meaning. Reading and talking with them every day is a treasure. And welcome to Chrisie and Austin's new baby, Tanner! Thanks for giving us a deadline we had to keep.

> *The human brain is a meaning-maker and meaning seeker.*
> —ERIC JENSEN

# CHAPTER
## 1

Leading with Meaning:
# DEVELOPING POSITIVE THEORIES OF READING

The act of seeking meaning leads each one of us to pick up a book, newspaper, or magazine or to read a blog or Facebook post. We read for enjoyment, to learn something new, to relax, to connect, and to get lost in the written word. These meaning-driven experiences with texts are universal and not unique to proficient adult readers. Chrisie's daughter Aubrey, like many young readers, is drawn to books in similar ways. At two years old, Aubrey has learned emotions and body parts from hearing lines like, "I love your happy side, your sad side, your silly side, your mad side" and "I love your fingers, and toes, your ears, and nose" in *I Love You Through and Through* (Rossetti-Shustak 2005). She bounces up and down as she enjoys the rhythm and rhyme in *Brown Bear, Brown Bear, What Do You See?* (Martin Jr. and Carle 1996). She shrieks in fear for the family in *Going on a Bear Hunt* when they approach the dark cave and the narrator describes the bear (Oxenbury and Rosen 1997). Daily interactions like these have led Aubrey to fall in love with reading and keep her climbing into Chrisie's lap multiple times a day chanting, "Mama, book! Mama, book!"

Many children enter school like Aubrey, seeing themselves as readers from the start. But for some, like Winston, a first grader, this identity starts to dissipate once they begin doing the print work for themselves. Winston doubts he is a successful reader, often saying, "I can't read" or "This book is too hard." To Winston, the reading he does at school seems to be different from the reading he experiences with his parents at home. The motivation and meaning that drive him to talk incessantly about snakes after hearing *I Don't Like Snakes* (Davies 2015) as a bedtime story slips away and his confidence is diminished when he reads books at school.

Classrooms are full of students like Winston and Aubrey, as well as children with a range of language and literacy experiences. We teach learners who excel as readers and we teach learners who are at the beginning of their English-language journey. We see students who find challenge in processing visual information at basic levels, and those who are reading Cynthia Rylant's *Poppleton* (1997) series in kindergarten. Regardless of their level of proficiency, all of these children seek to construct meaning and feel successful as they go about their day, and it's our job to make sure that happens. The joyful experiences of reading with our own children, and memories of being read to as a child, guide us to lead with meaning when we read with children in the classroom.

A multitude of school opportunities offer joyful encounters to understand texts: shared reading, interactive read-aloud, guided reading, independent reading, revisiting mentor texts, and creating relevant texts during writing workshop. Within each of these instructional methods, our actions as teachers can affect how students use their natural drive to seek meaning. This book takes a close look at one teaching component, guided reading, and narrows the scope even further by exploring how to plan the book introduction and facilitate the discussion segment of the lesson. We believe a well-crafted introduction has the power to guide readers in beginning to actively construct the meaning of the book even before they begin to read. This active construction of meaning before and during reading leads to authentic discussion after reading, which keeps the experience enjoyable and allows readers to negotiate meaning together.

Guided reading is a mainstay in comprehensive balanced literacy classrooms. It's a critical step in the gradual release of responsibility to students as they move from high levels of teacher support (e.g., interactive read-aloud and shared reading) to a low level of support (e.g., independent reading). In guided reading

- groups are small, dynamic, formed to address the needs of readers in the class, and adjusted as necessary based on the progress of each student;

- the teacher selects an appropriate book for the group—not too hard and not too easy, offering the right amount of instructional challenge;

- after the teacher orients the group to the book through the introduction, every child independently reads his or her own copy of the text while the teacher listens in and provides varying levels of instructional support;

- the students and teacher engage in discussion of the text once it's been read; and

- the teacher responds to the needs of the group with a teaching point that strengthens or extends the students' reading processing system, which is often followed by brief word work.

The elements of guided reading, when driven by responsive decision making from the teacher, prepare students to read successfully and lead them in the direction of understanding the text as deeply as possible. Responsive planning and teaching during guided reading is every bit as challenging as it is powerful. (See Figure 1.1 for professional texts that have guided our thinking in these areas.) Our intent in this book is to address these challenges by helping teachers develop habits of mind for planning that keep meaning at the core of instructional decisions. Let's begin by uncovering the child's perspective to explore how our actions might position readers. Then we can consider ways to shape our actions to positively affect how students view the act of reading.

Figure 1.1
RESOURCES FOR READING INSTRUCTION

**Assessment**
*Running Records: A Self-Tutoring Guide* by Peter Johnston (2000)
*Running Records for Classroom Teachers* by Marie Clay (2000)
*The Literacy Teacher's Playbook, Grades K–2* by Jennifer Serravallo (2014)
*Assessment in Perspective: Focusing on the Reader Behind the Numbers* by Clare Landrigan and Tammy Mulligan (2012)

**Guided Reading**
*Guided Reading: Responsive Teaching Across the Grades* by Irene Fountas and Gay Su Pinnell (2017b)

*(continues)*

*(continued)*

*Teaching for Comprehending and Fluency: Thinking, Talking, and Writing About Reading, K–8* by Irene C. Fountas and Gay Su Pinnell (2006)

**Making Teaching Points**
*Prompting Guide, Part 1 for Early Reading and Early Writing* by Irene C. Fountas and Gay Su Pinnell (2012)
*The Reading Strategies Book: Your Everything Guide to Developing Skilled Readers* by Jennifer Serravallo (2015)

**Talking About Text**
*Comprehension Through Conversation: The Power of Purposeful Talk in the Reading Workshop* by Maria Nichols (2006)
*Academic Conversations: Classroom Talk That Fosters Critical Thinking and Content Understandings* by Jeff Zwiers and Marie Crawford (2011)

**Working with Struggling Readers**
*When Readers Struggle: Teaching That Works* by Gay Su Pinnell and Irene C. Fountas and (2009)
*One Child at a Time: Making the Most of Your Time with Struggling Readers, K–6* by Pat Johnson (2006)
*Catching Readers Before They Fall: Supporting Readers Who Struggle, K–4* by Pat Johnson and Katie Keier (2010)
*Teaching Struggling Readers: Using Brain-Based Research to Maximize Learning* by Carol Lyons (2003)

## WHAT'S READING ABOUT? A CHILD'S PERSPECTIVE

Academics have explored theories of reading instruction for decades. The complexities of these theories have added layers to our understanding of reading instruction and uncovered more questions for us to explore. Here we explore the theory that the reader—each individual student in our class—holds about what reading is, the purposes of it, and how engaging with text serves personal purposes and goals. We want to study how a child's own theory affects how he or she reads and learns to read.

The theory a child holds may indicate how deeply he or she will engage in reading both in and outside of school and may determine how often he or she independently seeks out reading or perseveres with engaging yet challenging texts. We become concerned when students view reading as being "done to them" or as something they do because it's required rather than because it serves their own purposes. Supporting the whole child as a reader means considering each child's view of reading and in turn determining how our interactions may positively or negatively affect that view.

Kath's literacy coach once asked, "What is the child's theory of reading?" This question helps us interpret a student's reading behaviors to reveal his or her current reading theory. Some children, like Aubrey, may enter school with a solid understanding that books are pleasurable and full of meaning, that readers talk about books they love, and that readers have opinions about books and favorites they like to revisit. Others, like Winston, may think that school reading just means getting the words right or remembering all the events to retell to the teacher. Classroom and testing situations, home interactions, bedtime stories, discussions of ideas—each scenario has the potential to contribute to a child's theory of reading, positively or otherwise, regardless of intention.

As teachers, we have control only over what goes on in our classrooms. As such, how we engage children with text—how we listen and respond to them—contributes to their identities as readers (and as writers and learners) and to how they perceive what reading can do for them. Even how we introduce a book or set up a conversation about a text contributes to a child's evolving theory. Recognizing that power is as exciting as it is daunting.

## HIERARCHY OF MEANING

During a coaching session a few years ago, Tina Henry of The Ohio State University scribbled on the back of her notepad and then held up a quick sketch to illustrate Marie Clay's (1991) hierarchy of written language (see Figure 1.2).

Figure 1.2
HIERARCHY OF WRITTEN LANGUAGE

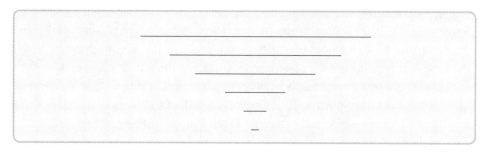

She then explained that the top line represents the meaning of the entire book, the next line represents meaning at the chapter, scene, or page level, then the paragraph, the sentence, the word, and the letter. Ultimately, the purpose of reading is to come away with an understanding of the text as a whole (the top line). As proficient readers, how we construct meaning of the "top line" is not linear. We may start with an idea of the greater meaning, move down to work within a subset, and then shift back up to the bigger picture. We constantly return to larger, more comprehensive units of meaning. For example, working to figure out an unknown word, we may reread to regain the meaning of the sentence and then put it in context of the whole book. Similarly, a character's series of actions in a scene (the second line) can reveal the motivation of the character, which is central to the meaning of the entire story (the top line). In *Henry and Mudge in Puddle Trouble*, when Henry whispers to Mudge that he *needs* to pick the snow glory that his parents told him not to, we recognize the tension of wanting something badly and not being able to have it (Rylant 1996). So, we empathize with Henry's decision to succumb to the urge to take what he shouldn't have. Understanding this scene contributes to our understanding of how Henry's character develops in the whole story. In this way, readers work to use the smaller bits of information to appraise their understanding of the whole. As teachers, we keep this hierarchy of written language in mind while interacting with students so that the final outcome for them is to comprehend at the top line. (We will refer to the hierarchy of written language throughout the book.)

# BOOK INTRODUCTIONS: DOORWAYS TO MEANING-MAKING

Powerful introductions serve as doorways, leading students down the path of actively constructing meaning. Effective book introductions ground readers' thinking and teach them how to use meaning to develop a rich understanding on their own.

Recently, when our division's central office was reorganized, we had new opportunities to collaborate with colleagues we've never met. On one such project, Suzanne was paired up with Stephanie. Beforehand, she was told that Stephanie was smart and professional, that she was calm, that she listened well, and that she thought about how things fit into the bigger picture; in short, that she would love working with her. Because Suzanne had not yet met Stephanie, this "introduction" shaped her first impression. During their initial meeting, Suzanne was on the lookout for evidence of the attributes she'd been told about. As it turned out, Stephanie was every bit as professional and intelligent as described. With each subsequent encounter, Suzanne was tuned to Stephanie's sparks of intellect and professionalism, which goes to show how much introductions work to shape thinking in powerful ways.

Learning how to strategically plan for book introductions will expand our understandings of texts, the reading process, and teaching moves. While it would be convenient to pick up a teacher's guide and deliver a prescribed book introduction, the most important element—the students sitting before us—would be missing from the equation. Reading progress sometimes plateaus when we follow a scripted plan based on the text, rather than including each of the students' unique strengths and needs in the planning.

The other important element in the equation is the teacher. Our decisions affect how we interpret reading behaviors, select texts, use language to guide students, and more. Though preplanned, introductions must retain an element of improvisation, with teachers making in-the-moment tweaks in response to what the students say and do. These interactions

- shape the learners' theories of reading,

- focus on meaning,

- support problem solving,

- promote deep thinking, and

- foster discussion with others.

Let's think about how our teaching language and conversational moves shape students' first impressions of text. We'll start with a hypothetical traditional interaction, more of a "picture walk" than a book introduction, between a teacher and a group of first graders, and their subsequent discussion after the reading.

| TEACHER | This is a book called *Billy Can Count* (Giles 2000). It's about two brothers, Jack and Billy. There's Jack, who is the older brother, and Billy, who is the younger brother. Let's look at the pictures and see what's happening in the story. (*Teacher and students open to pages 2 and 3.*) |
|---|---|
| S1 | Mom and Jack got the bowls. |
| S2 | There's yellow, and green, and orange, and blue. |
| TEACHER | Turn to pages 4 and 5. Now what do you see? |
| S3 | She gave spoons to the little boy. |
| TEACHER | (*Turns to pages 6 and 7.*) And look what happens here. Jack and Billy are setting the table for dinner. Do you set the table at your house? |
| S4 | Yeah, sometimes. |
| S2 | Not really. (*Interaction continues to follow this pattern as students are asked to look at pages 8–15 and tell what they see in the pictures. The last page is kept "hidden" so as not to reveal the ending.*) |
| TEACHER | There are a couple of words you need to know before you read this book. (*Holds up whiteboard and writes and says the words* looked, bowls, *and* spoons. *Students repeat the words after the teacher.*) Now you'll know these words when you see them in your book. If you forget, you can look back up here and remember. Now it's time to read to find out if Billy learns to count! |

Students read the text while the teacher listens in and makes individual teaching points. The teacher then reconvenes the group for a discussion.

| TEACHER | So, did Billy learn how to count? |
|---|---|
| S2 | Yes, at the end. |
| TEACHER | What happened first? |

| S3 | Jack counted the bowls but Billy didn't count right. |
|---|---|
| TEACHER | And then what happened? |
| S1 | Jack showed him how to count, but he did it all crazy, like one, two, six, ten. |
| TEACHER | And what happened after that? (*Interaction continues as students retell the events in sequence.*) |

Because the teacher's introduction directed students to attend at the word and page level, the students' interactions with the text remained at that level. Think about the subtle messages this well-intentioned teacher may have sent to her students:

- All the meaning is in the pictures.

- You should remember a tricky word if I show it to you.

- If you don't know a word, take your eyes and attention out of the book to look at the word on the whiteboard and see if that helps you remember.

- Thinking and talking about books means retelling them in order, detail by detail.

We, too, have led this type of interaction, directing students to talk about what they see page by page and commenting together on the illustrations. We stopped using this approach, as well as the term *picture walk*, because we don't want to send the message (to ourselves *or* to students) that meaning is conveyed solely through pictures or that it is always constructed at the page level, in sequence, one page at a time. Sure, there is value in searching for meaning in the illustrations and photographs in service of understanding the text, but as Fountas and Pinnell remind us, "the introduction is *not* a 'picture walk'—it is about orienting the reader to the meaning of the whole text" (2009, 409). We may not need to look at every picture to do this. We want children to understand that in reading, the whole is greater than the sum of its parts. The parts in a book connect with each other, allowing readers to comprehend at a deeper level.

Consider the experience of one of Kath's former students, a first grader named Helen, as she was reading *The Hungry Kitten* (Randell 1996) for the first time. She paused before starting every new page and gave a sigh of relief at the end of each page. She read word by word. When she finished, her response was basic and recounted one of the last events in the story: "The boy gave the kitten some milk." By looking at the notes on Helen's reading behaviors, Kath and her coach surmised that she was reading at the page level—working hard to read the words on each page without tying the pages together to construct the saga of a very hungry and very lonely kitten that must fend for himself.

Looking back at the transcript of her book introduction, Kath and her coach noticed that it was designed as a page-by-page preview: students discussed the characters in each scene and talked about unknown words. There was no meaningful thread to help Helen tie the story together. This is a common misstep. Sometimes we're so concerned about supporting students with new words that we forget to help them see the importance of connecting the events in a story. Instead, what we should do during the introduction is enable students to begin building understandings of the "top line" of the hierarchy of written language to serve as support for the problem solving they will do at all levels as they read.

Now, consider the following excerpt from an actual book introduction and the messages our colleague Suzanne Fisher may be sending to her first graders about reading:

| MS. FISHER | I have a new book for you today called *Billy Can Count.* Remember Jack and Billy? Well, in this story, Mom made soup for dinner for herself, Dad, Jack, and Billy. Jack and Billy need to get the table ready. They need to get the bowls and the spoons for everyone. Remember which is the big brother? |
|---|---|
| ANTHONY | Jack |
| MS. FISHER | That's right. This is Jack and he already knows how to count. But Billy is little. |
| ANTHONY | He doesn't know how to count. (*Giggles.*) |
| MS. FISHER | They set out the bowls and spoons and need to make sure that everyone in the family gets one. Look, in this part (*pages 2 and 3*), Mom gives Jack the bowls. Look at how many bowls she gives him. |
| MICHELLE | Four. |
| MS. FISHER | Yes, and he counts them one, two, three, four. (*Kids join in.*) Turn to page 4. Mom gives Billy . . . |
| MICHELLE | Forks! No, I mean . . . |

| KIM | Spoons. |
|---|---|
| MS. FISHER | Yes, she gives Billy spoons, and when he tries to count them, look at what he says! (*Points to text.*) |
| ALL | One, two, six, ten! (*Students giggle.*) |
| ANTHONY | He doesn't know how to count. |
| KIM | He did it funny. (*Giggles.*) |
| MS. FISHER | It is funny. You want to say it again? |
| ALL | One, two, six, ten! (*Laughter.*) |
| MS. FISHER | Billy doesn't know how to count yet, so Jack has to think of a way to teach Billy how to count. |
| MICHELLE | (*Flipping to the last page.*) He did it! |
| MS. FISHER | He finally did it! As you're reading, think about how hard Jack works to help Billy learn how to count. |

Students read the text while Suzanne listened in and made individual teaching points. She reconvened the group for a discussion.

| MS. FISHER | Jack worked really hard to teach Billy how to count. |
|---|---|
| ANTHONY | It was funny, the way he said it. |
| MICHELLE | I have a question about Billy. Billy don't know how to count because he's little and that's why Jack showed him to count. |
| MS. FISHER | He showed him by putting out the bowls, right? What does that make you think about the type of brother Jack is? |
| MICHELLE | He's a good one. |
| ANTHONY | I want this book. |
| MS. FISHER | You'll get it for your book box! (*To Kim.*) What are you thinking, Kim? |
| KIM | I think Billy doesn't know how to count. In the end, Jack taught him how to count in this page (*page 10*) when Billy set the spoons for Mom, Dad, Jack, and Billy. And then he counts and then he did it. |
| MS. FISHER | He probably felt so proud of himself for showing Billy that. (*To Anthony.*) Does your big brother teach you things? |
| ANTHONY | Not really. |

| MS. FISHER | No? (*To Michelle.*) I bet you teach your little brother. |
|---|---|
| MICHELLE | I teach my little brother. And he count like this: one, two, three, seventeen, and I said, "That's not like that!" He needs to say one, two, three, four, but he still can't do it! |
| KIM | Is he too little? |
| MICHELLE | Yes! |

By focusing on a bigger idea—Jack helping his younger brother—in her introduction, Suzanne set the students' minds up for thinking at the top line of the hierarchy of written language. She kept the focus on constructing meaning as she sent them off to read independently by launching them with this bigger idea and then returning to it during the discussion.

The interactions between Suzanne and her students may have conveyed the following messages:

- What you already know can help you understand and think about books.

- It's important to think about the story as you read.

- What you think is valued.

- There isn't always one right way to think about text.

- You can know the ending of a book and still think about and enjoy reading it.

- Characters say funny things that are fun to repeat.

These messages support the growth of positive emotions and theories toward reading. Imagine how, over time, this type of interaction shapes the quality of students' talk and the depth of their thinking. Additionally, Anthony, Michelle, and Kim have a clear sense that reading is about enjoyment and constructing something meaningful that adds value to their lives.

Book introductions like Suzanne Fisher's are intentional and instructional, yet relaxed and enjoyable. She knows what supports the children need and uses that information to plan—from text selection, to supporting students with challenges in the text, to crafting an opening statement that supports constructing a big idea. During a book introduction, Suzanne is active and deliberate. The students are also active and focused on thinking about the content of the book. Suzanne's example illustrates how the interactions we have in the first few moments can set students up to become the type of readers who can discuss more than just the information explicitly stated in the text. Our planned teaching moves may not always be precisely on target, but when we focus on meaning, we are always heading in the right direction.

## CRAFTING EFFECTIVE BOOK INTRODUCTIONS

Book introductions are most effective when each component (Figure 1.3) sets students up to actively search for, use, and expand meaning.

Figure 1.3
STRUCTURE OF A BOOK INTRODUCTION

Text Selection and Analysis
(Done before introducing the text to students.)

Overall Meaning Statement

Support with Challenging Characteristics
(when necessary)

- Text Structures

- Language Structures

- Words

- Other Features

Launching Statement/Question

Our colleague Shele Banford helps us visualize the structure of a book introduction by comparing it to an hourglass. We start broad with a meaning statement that provides an overall introduction to what the book is about, narrow the focus to smaller units of meaning at structural and word levels, and then return to the broader meaning with a launching statement or question that gets readers thinking about bigger ideas. Subsequent chapters will explore each of these components in depth by describing options, decisions, and examples of planning processes and book introductions.

## Text Selection and Analysis (Chapter 2)

Although selecting and analyzing texts isn't technically part of the introduction, the process is fundamental for ensuring that students construct meaning while they read. We start with our students in mind—their interests, instructional level, strengths, and needs. Keeping students at the forefront guides us toward selecting a text that will engage, support, and challenge them.

## Overall Meaning Statement (Chapter 3)

Once we've selected a text, closer analysis helps us move beyond what the book is about (literal-level meaning) to get at possibilities of deeper meaning or big ideas. Uncovering the layers of what a text might mean to the readers reminds us to consider students' perspectives and introduce texts in a manner that draws their attention to the top line of the hierarchy of written language. Just as we read the back-cover blurb to get a feel for what a book will be about, we begin guided reading introductions with similar "blurbs" for our students. Only a few brief sentences, the overall meaning statement draws students into the text, provides them with a frame for thinking to help them construct the meaning of the text, and often leads to a brief conversation with students.

## Launching Statement/Question (Chapter 3)

Book introductions begin with meaning and then dip down into sub-layers—text structure, language structures, and words. Since comprehension is the heart and soul of reading, the very last thing we say to students should pop them back up to the top of the meaning hierarchy before they begin to read. We've begun to refer to our last statement to students during the book introduction as a launching statement, which sets their minds again toward constructing the meaning of the text. Crafting the launching statement is easiest while you're analyzing the text for meaning, so we discuss launching statements in Chapter 3. In real time, when you are engaging students in a book introduction, it is the last thing you say, just before students begin to read their individual copies of the text.

## Support with Challenging Characteristics (Chapters 4, 5, 6)

It is likely that students will need support with text characteristics when we introduce them to texts at their instructional level. Analyzing a text in relation to what we know about the readers helps us make decisions about what we might need to "debug" to help them have a successful first read. We consider text structures, language structures, words, and other features, always asking ourselves: *What is already known or familiar to students? What do we think students can figure out on their own and what can be left for reading work? What do we need to explicitly introduce?* These essential questions help us monitor the level of support we provide for students without taking away opportunities for them to problem-solve on their own. Chapters 4, 5, and 6 break down the process of analyzing several different characteristics of text: overarching text structures, language structures, and words (identification, decoding, and vocabulary). Through excerpts of book introductions, you'll see that even when we dip down into explaining how a book works, for example, we do so by connecting it to meaning.

Since each chapter takes on a different characteristic, planning a book introduction can seem overwhelming and time-consuming. It's important to remember—and we reiterate this point throughout the book—that the teacher will need to decide which of these characteristics to introduce based on the needs of the students in the group. Our goal is to help you consider possibilities of what might need to be supported and how you might support students during introductions, not to suggest that everything has to be covered during them. After all, book introductions should be brief and efficient so that kids spend most of the lesson reading!

## Discussion (Chapter 7)

Readers need a chance to authentically respond to what they read. In a guided reading lesson, this conversation may last only a few minutes, but they're a very important few minutes. Since reading is about making meaning, we make it a habit to return to, build on, and listen for evidence of meaning through discussion immediately after students finish reading. We've included Chapter 7 to help you think about what's worth talking about with readers, structures and routines to establish, and ways to facilitate powerful conversations.

## GO SLOW TO GO FAST

When it comes to developing habits for planning, it pays to slow down, attend to our thinking, and notice what we're doing and why we're doing it. By taking time to closely analyze our actions up front, we better understand the rationales behind our work. This helps create habits of mind that eventually become second nature to us.

The same is true for learning many things in life. Take Zumba, the high-energy dance workout, as an example. Instructors at Chrisie's gym typically introduce a new routine every month or so. During the first week, and periodically throughout the month, the instructor introduces an eight-count segment in slow motion and provides verbal cues as a scaffold. The class rehearses parts of the routine a few times, also in slow motion, paying close attention to foot placement, turns, and unique moves. Then, the instructor cranks up the music and everyone jams! Taking the time to go slow at first helps everyone become more automatic with their moves so that their attention is eventually freed up to refine their technique, incorporate their own style, and enjoy the class more. While slowing things down week after week would neither be necessary nor a good use of time, it is needed up front for the class participants to "go fast" and effectively integrate all the intricate moves involved later on their own.

Similarly, we invite you to "go slow to go fast" with us throughout this book as we analyze texts, plan book introductions, and prepare for meaningful conversations. In the following chapters, we carefully break down the planning process to support our young readers as they think their way through a text and discuss it after reading. As you go through this process, you might find yourself thinking, "There isn't enough time for me to plan like this for every group, every day!" And we'd agree. What you will find is that just as Chrisie's metacognitive awareness of foot placement and direction became habitual and automatic, so too will your awareness of how you think and plan when you pick up a text that you are about to introduce. You might find that it takes only a few attempts to internalize this process. You might also find that you return to this slowed-down process as you work with a group of struggling readers who need more attention or support a group of students who seem to have plateaued in their growth. This process may also help you think through introducing new levels or genres or whenever you feel the need to reflect on and refine your planning and instruction.

Imagine a group of kids coming to the guided reading table as enthusiastically as Aubrey when she crawls onto Chrisie's lap saying, "Mama, book!" Picture students so comfortable and confident that they lean forward, itching to grab the book out of the teacher's hand, eager to discover what's inside, and then excited to talk with others about what they think.

Now imagine that you have the power to influence how your students perceive themselves as readers. You do. Effective teaching is a series of complex decisions. Our hope is that this book helps you adopt ways of thinking to guide this complex decision-making process—ways that result in young readers becoming powerful meaning-makers.

*The goal should always be to give the right book, at the right time, to the right child. That's how we make lifelong readers who not only can read, but want to read.*

—JANICE HARRINGTON (2012)

# CHAPTER
# 2

# Kids First:
# MATCHING READERS WITH TEXTS

Have you ever been twelve minutes into a guided reading lesson when you realize there is no way you'll be able to finish because you're still introducing the text? Have you ever found yourself spending ten minutes to introduce a book that takes students about three minutes to read? If so, you may have fallen victim to the "maxi-intro." This phenomenon generally occurs because we are either trying to teach too much in the text or the text we selected is just too hard. This situation can usually be avoided by knowing our readers and effectively matching them with books that keep them at the cutting edge of their competencies, enabling them to effectively process, or read, the text on their own.

We can't—and shouldn't—try to teach everything in the book introduction. We want to ensure that students have a successful first read, and we want to make sure they have reading work to do that nudges them to grow as readers. That's quite a challenge! But the better we know our kids as readers and the better we know the books we introduce to them, the easier our planning and teaching, and ultimately student learning, become.

## TEXT LEVELS: MERELY A STARTING POINT

Matching books with readers is a lot like shoe shopping. Chrisie recently facilitated a full-day workshop and needed some new shoes to go with the outfit she planned to wear. As she started her shopping excursion, she walked into the shoe store and made a beeline for the eight-and-a-half section to begin her search. Since she was going to be on her feet all day, it was critical that her shoes be comfortable. She likes to be fashionable, so they also had to be stylish. Knowing that the pants she was going to wear were a little long, the shoes she wanted to have a slight heel, preferably a wedge, for more support. Needless to say, she couldn't just grab the first pair she saw in her size; otherwise, she would have risked a painful day of stumbling around in four-inch stilettos, or feeling comfortable yet ridiculous in shoes that had her looking like her grandmother.

Having criteria during the search helped Chrisie quickly scan the shelves and find some contenders. It wasn't enough to just look at their outward appearance: she had to get the shoes out of their boxes and inspect them a little more closely. She analyzed characteristics: whether or not the color would work, whether they were too wide or too narrow, too tight or too loose, flexible or stiff, the heel too high or too short. These criteria allowed her to narrow her options until she found a pair that matched the occasion, enabling her to have a stylish yet comfortable day on her feet.

Just as size is merely a starting point when shoe shopping, text levels are merely a starting point when we are "shopping" for books to use in guided reading. We closely inspect books that might be a good fit for our instructional purpose at a particular point in time. Keeping students' interests, strengths, and needs in mind, we envision the type of book that will "match the occasion" by providing just the right amount of support and challenge. We don't arbitrarily grab a book at students' level and think, "Hmm, what can I teach from this book today?" Just as not all shoes of the same size will match the same occasion, neither will all texts at a given level.

We foster successful reading experiences when we thoughtfully match readers with books. In this chapter, we discuss how to make a good match by exploring

- rationales to support the use of instructional-level texts;

- a process for thoughtfully selecting texts:

- o  connecting with readers;

- o  identifying characteristics of texts that will support and challenge students;

- o  selecting the best next book; and

- pulling it all together: a case study.

## THE CASE FOR USING HIGH-QUALITY INSTRUCTIONAL-LEVEL TEXTS

Chrisie once trained for a half-marathon. A self-proclaimed nonrunner, she looked up one of those "couch to half" training plans online and was shocked that her current ability was far behind what the training plan recommended for her time line. After panicking a bit, she called for help from her friend Meghann, an experienced marathon runner. The first thing Meghann said was, "Sure, I'll help. Let's go for a run together. You set the pace and distance and I'll just follow along." This initial run (let's be honest, a brief jog/walk combo) gave Meghann the chance to observe Chrisie's stride, notice her breathing and how she used her arms, and determine when she started running out of steam. Afterward, she gave Chrisie a few pointers and sat her down to create a short-term training plan based on her observations. Chrisie worried that this plan conflicted with what she had read online.

"The plan says I should be running twice as far as you're suggesting!" she said.

Meghann smiled. "But that plan doesn't know you," she said. "Let's start with where you are and build from there. We'll increase your distance by about 10 percent this week and then we'll reevaluate. When your runs start to feel too easy or comfortable, we'll up the ante. When you're feeling challenged but still mostly enjoying your runs, we'll know you're in your sweet spot."

Meghann knew that if Chrisie started with the "one-size-fits-all" schedule, regardless of her current fitness level, she likely would fail miserably—quitting because of injury or lack of success or motivation. The training would be too hard. Instead, Meghann started at a place where Chrisie was successful yet challenged, and matched her with a plan that moved her forward, regularly increasing the distance and intensity as she built stamina along the way.

A few months later, Chrisie reached her goal: crossing the finish line after running 13.1 miles!

We start with our readers the same way Meghann started with Chrisie—figuring out what they can do before creating a feasible yet rigorous plan. The trick is finding the sweet spot—what Lev Vygotsky (1978) called the "zone of proximal development"—so that the reader feels success while also being stretched to tackle something new. As Marie Clay wrote, "The teaching should not start where the teacher (or program) is but where the child is!" (2005, 32). That's a tall order for us as teachers, especially when we have twenty or more students to think about, but when we make a habit of using what we know about our students as a guide, we maximize the potential for student engagement and reading progress.

Developing readers, like developing runners, acquire different skills in a different order at a different pace. Teachers are like coaches: we regularly keep an eye on what children are learning in order to best match readers with a text (just as the coach may change the distance, pace, or location of the run). Ideally, a text has the perfect level of challenge to keep readers moving on an upward trajectory. To make this match, teachers engage in frequent formative assessment by observing students' reading behaviors—what we see them do while they read. We take running records or anecdotal notes, writing down substituted words, corrected errors, or what students do while problem solving. (See Figure 2.1 for information on running records.) These observations guide us to adjust instructional text levels so that we stay within students' ever-shifting range of reading development.

The guidelines from most reading experts suggest that students are working within their instructional level when they read books with 90–94 percent accuracy and at least satisfactory comprehension. We keep a close eye on students as their reading processing system develops and typically increase the challenge when they start to read above 94 percent accuracy while maintaining or strengthening comprehension. Without ongoing assessments, we run the risk that students will plateau because the level of challenge hasn't increased with their growing proficiency—or even worse, that we will cause unnecessary struggle, a distaste for reading, or a negative view of their own reading ability if we work outside their zone of proximal development.

Figure 2.1
ASSESSING READERS WITH RUNNING RECORDS

## Running Records

**What?** Running records are formative assessments that provide both quantitative and qualitative information about a child's observable reading behaviors. Administered individually, the record provides a visual representation of how a child uses meaning, structure, and visual information, his percentage of accuracy, and self-correction ratio or number of self-corrections. After reading, the child is engaged in conversation about what was read, providing a glimpse into how he comprehended the text.

**Why?** Running records are crucial tools that help drive a teacher's instructional decision making and monitor students' progress. After analyzing the running record, the information gleaned supports decisions about grouping, text selection, and future instruction.

**Who?** Running records are administered on a regular rotating basis for children reading around level J and below, less frequently (once a month or on an as-needed basis) for children reading at higher levels. For instance, if there are five students in a group and a new book is introduced each lesson, the teacher would take a running record on one student per book, gathering a record for everyone in the group every five lessons.

**When?** The running record is taken on the child's second read of the book to see how the student independently processes the text and serves to check how well the child is taking on the teacher's instruction. This typically occurs at the beginning of the next guided reading lesson (while others in the group reread books) or at another time during the day. Running records are most beneficial when analyzed and used to guide next steps in instruction.

If you find the management of coding, scoring, and analyzing running records to be a challenge, you may consider setting short-term goals for yourself. For example, focus on three

*(continues)*

*(continued)*

students. Take and analyze one running record for each student, for three weeks in a row, and look for signs of progress. Then focus on another group of students.

**How?** The teacher uses a standard coding system (Clay 2000) to record a child's reading behaviors while that child reads aloud to her. The teacher remains a neutral observer and does not teach or prompt the student as he or she reads. After the record is taken, the teacher makes one or two teaching points based on her observations and follows guidelines to score and analyze the record.

## A Few Notes About Texts Used for Guided Reading

Working in students' zones of proximal development and selecting and sequencing books from a robust collection of leveled texts will be the most responsive approach to instruction. We offer a few considerations here for using texts that represent grade-level expectations, avoiding texts that are too hard for guided reading, and what to do when selecting and sequencing texts isn't an option.

### Reading Texts That Represent Grade-Level Expectations

Some educators believe that children should be instructed only with texts that represent grade-level expectations to maintain rigor in the classroom. We'd rather advocate for a balanced diet of reading opportunities. We, too, believe that all students, regardless of their instructional levels, should have opportunities to interact with grade-level-appropriate texts, especially when provided with support as needed (e.g., interactive read-aloud, shared reading, or online audiobooks). We also believe that all students should have the opportunity to be met where they will learn best—at their instructional level. Based on the individual's proficiency, this level may dip below or rise above grade-level expectations.

Richard Allington's review of the research supports this thinking. He and his colleagues concluded that instructional texts that can be read with high accuracy produce greater gains than more difficult texts read with lower accuracy (Allington, McCuiston, and Billen 2015). Put simply, kids learn better when the reading isn't too hard. All students deserve to have numerous interactions with books that help them grow as readers without being so hard that they struggle or so easy that they disengage.

## When the Text Is Too Hard

Think about your own reading proficiency for a moment. You likely consider yourself to be an adept reader; you read most words with ease and accuracy, comprehend what is read on various levels, and sound fluent when reading aloud. Now, take a moment to read aloud the following excerpt from a medical publication abstract on nucleic acids research:

> *Combinatorial gene regulation largely contributes to phenotypic versatility in higher eukaryotes. Genome-wide chromatin immuno-precipitation (ChIP) combined with expression profiling can dissect regulatory circuits around transcriptional regulators. Here, we integrate tiling array measurements of DNA-binding sites for c-Myc, sp1, TFIID and modified histones with a tissue expression atlas to establish the functional correspondence between physical binding, promoter activity and transcriptional regulation. For this we develop SLM, a methodology to map c-Myc and sp1-binding sites and then classify sites as sp1-only, c-Myc-only or dual. (Parisi, Wirapati, and Naef 2007)*

Though we couldn't hear or see you, we're willing to bet you exhibited several of the following behaviors: spurts of dysfluent reading, "sounding out" words, rereading with a puzzled look on your face, leaning in closer to the text, and maybe even giving up and putting your head down on the table in exhaustion. Our guess is that you also don't have a clue about the literal meaning of the passage, let alone what any deeper understandings may be.

Think about what we just did. We had the power to turn you, a proficient reader, into a reader who struggled, merely through our text selection. As teachers, we have the power to do the same to our students. Our hunch is that even if we gave you an introduction to the paragraph on nucleic acids, there would still be too many unknown concepts for you to truly understand what it is about and reading it would consequently be fruitless. The text is just too hard. Our goal is to avoid making students struggle through guided reading texts by selecting books at students' current instructional level and providing enough support so that they can competently read and understand them.

### When Selecting and Sequencing Texts for Instruction Isn't an Option

Selecting from a body of high-quality text is the most responsive way to build on students' strengths and meet their needs. However, we recognize that some schools use programs with texts that have been preselected and sequenced by a publisher. In these cases, we suggest conducting frequent ongoing assessment and regularly adjusting students' placements within the publisher's suggested sequence. It is still critical to lead instruction with what you know about your students' strengths, needs, and reading preferences. This information can guide your introduction to the text, inform the teaching interactions you make as students read, and set the stage for how you engage students in discussion of the text after they read it.

## LOOKING BEYOND THE LEVEL: GETTING TO KNOW OUR READERS

When Chrisie was shoe shopping, it wasn't enough for her to grab any pair in her size. She had to examine the characteristics and select a pair that met her criteria. In the same way, we use characteristics of texts based on a set of criteria that arises from what we know about our students.

The following planning frame uses what we know about our students to choose the most effective texts for instruction:

> **IF** I have evidence that suggests [*students' interests, strengths, and needs based on their reading behaviors*] . . .
>
> **THEN** I'll select a book that [*characteristics of texts that will offer opportunities to build on identified strengths and support identified needs*].

This sequence prioritizes what's most important in every instructional scenario: our students. Only when we clearly understand who they are as readers and what they need next can we choose texts that will support their growth toward independence.

What follows is a three-step process for matching readers with books. The first, getting to know our readers (the IF), is of utmost importance and fully guides the next two steps: developing criteria for text selection and determining instructional value to select the next best book (the THEN).

## Step 1: Getting to Know Our Readers

Who are our students as readers? We want our students to enjoy reading, develop healthy theories of what reading is all about, and feel successful yet challenged as they read, so we invest in time to get to know them well. We gather information about our readers to help us reach these goals by asking three simple questions:

- What do they **like**?

- What do they **do**?

- How do they **think**?

You'll find that the formal and informal data you collect and analyze as you repeatedly ask yourself these questions throughout the year completes the first part of the planning frame, "If I have evidence that suggests..." When we have strong evidence to support the first part of the equation, we find that it is easier for us to identify criteria to use as we select books for students. This, in turn, helps us narrow down options of texts that will have significant instructional value for them.

### *What Do Readers Like?*

Personal interests are vast. Texts can enhance interests that readers already hold as well as expand interests, providing windows into other worlds and ways of being. Ultimately, texts have the power to motivate or deter readers.

Chrisie's husband, Austin, now an avid reader, hated to read as a kid; the books his teachers gave him were, in his words, "just plain boring." As an adult, he discovered *John Adams* by David McCullough, which set him on the path to reading for pleasure. Austin's experience with this book was so powerful that he gained a favorite author (he has read every David McCullough book), became interested in biographies (his bookshelves are full of them), and expanded his reading horizons to other genres (he now loves historical fiction as well as narrative and expository nonfiction).

Austin's experience echoes those of many of our students: to appreciate the value and pleasure of reading, he needed a book that deeply engaged him. Too many students spend too much time reading lackluster passages on worksheets or low-quality books with disengaging story lines, characters, and topics. We can't just put words in front of kids and expect them to become self-motivated readers. We must give them something worth reading—something they can relate to, learn from, enjoy, and dive into wholeheartedly. It's our responsibility to make that happen early and often so that our students learn to love reading now and don't miss out on the power of what reading can do for them throughout their life.

So, how do we learn about our students' reading preferences? By talking with them and observing how they react to books, of course! A reading interest inventory with questions such as *What types of books do you like to read? Who are your favorite authors?* and *Why do you like to read?* may be helpful to find out what, where, when, why, and with whom students like to read.

You can also find out this information informally, and more authentically, by engaging in intentional conversations with students: *What are you thinking about these characters? Why did you pick this book? What are you planning to read next? I learned so much about this topic, what about you? Who else might like to read this? Why?* Ask, listen, and ask more. Eavesdrop on conversations that kids have with their peers during partner talk and share time, and take note of the books they return to and the ones with which they seem most engaged. Pay attention to the types of books that make them laugh, ask questions, and talk about ideas. Notice which books lead to other book choices and which books students want read aloud again. Your observations and students' responses lead to characteristics you can search for when matching them with books: humor, engaging illustrations, topics of interest, characters in a series, and more.

## What Do Readers Do?

While knowing students' instructional levels is helpful for matching readers with books, the level itself isn't enough on its own. We must look beyond the level to learn *how* a child reads if we are to gain insights that drive our instruction. Marie Clay explains: "Compare this to a football game; the quality of the team play is not improved by looking at the final score. Rather, the coach must look closely at how the team is playing the game and help the players use strategic moves which produce a better final score" (2013, 7). We gain a stronger sense of how our readers are "playing the game" when we closely attend to what they *do* while reading. We notice how they figure out unknown words, what they do after they make an error, how their reading sounds, and other actions they take. As we become aware of how they process text, we look for patterns in their reading behaviors to infer strengths that can be built upon in addition to needs for next steps in instruction.

Using running records (see Figure 2.1) to record and analyze a student's observable reading behaviors is the most authentic and effective way to learn what readers do as they read. If running records are not yet a part of your assessing and teaching repertoire, you can still gather a great deal of information by taking anecdotal notes on what you observe students do as they read, as well as on the contributions they make during conversations about books. All these observations serve as a window into what students can do, can almost do, and may need to learn to do next. Figure 2.2 includes questions to guide your analysis of what you observe.

Figure 2.2
QUESTIONS TO GUIDE ANALYSIS OF OBSERVABLE READING BEHAVIORS

What do I notice about the readers' stretches of accurate reading (long versus short stretches, rereading, fluency)?

What, if anything, do readers do at the point of difficulty (stop, appeal to the teacher, check the picture, reread, make the sound of the first letters, break a word into parts)?

How consistently do readers notice (monitor) when they have made an error (hesitate, stop, appeal to the teacher)? What do they do once they've noticed they've made an error (self-correct at the point of error, reread, make another attempt, read on)?

How does their reading sound? To what extent do they read in meaningful phrases? Read with appropriate momentum? Use punctuation to guide their reading? Read with intonation and inflection in their voice? Apply appropriate stress on words and phrases?

## How Do Readers Think?

The reading behaviors mentioned above can often be directly observed, and they provide clues about how readers solve problems and check on themselves as they read. Other behaviors occur strictly in the head and are impossible to see, but are just as important to uncover because they provide insight into how students construct understandings of the text.

To get a picture of how students think about or comprehend texts, we engage in conversational exchanges with them and listen intently to their comments. These conversations have a give-and-take quality to them and occur throughout the day during interactive read-alouds, reading conferences, and book clubs as well as after guided reading. Questions are asked, thoughts are shared, ideas are agreed with, challenged, and built upon. We listen for evidence of how students put ideas together and summarize what they've read, connect to the text in various ways, predict what may happen, infer meaning beyond what the author explicitly states, join previously held ideas with new ones to arrive at new or deeper understandings, notice aspects of the way the author crafted the text, and form opinions about what they read. As we reflect on these conversations, we ask ourselves the questions in Figure 2.3 to infer what students' comments reveal about the way they construct understandings so that we can learn what to teach and how to support.

Figure 2.3
QUESTIONS TO GUIDE ANALYSIS OF "IN THE HEAD" READING BEHAVIORS

What do students' comments reveal about the way they

- summarize the main points of what they've read?

- predict what might happen?

- connect what they know about their life, other books, and the world around them with what is happening in the text? Use these connections to deepen understanding of the text?

- infer meaning (feelings, motivations, themes) beyond what is explicitly stated?

- synthesize previously held understandings with new ones?

- notice, use, and appreciate the author's crafting moves?

- form and share opinions about what they liked and didn't like about a text?

Once we consider what students like, what they do, and how they think (**IF**), we can begin working to select a book that will be a good fit for them (**THEN**). To illustrate the process, we follow Chrisie as she got to know a group of first-grade readers. We then move through the next two steps as she established the criteria of what to look for in a text and selected the next book for instruction.

## CASE STUDY: A FIRST-GRADE GROUP

Four first graders—Maria, Marvin, Ricky, and Sarah—were working together in a guided reading group and reading instructionally at level E. When Chrisie closely analyzed their running records and anecdotal notes and asked herself the questions in Figures 2.2 and 2.3, she began to see patterns emerge in the actions these readers took while reading and thinking about texts. These patterns led her to uncover students' strengths that she could build upon and determine needs for next steps in instruction.

### Step 1: Getting to Know Our Readers

Starting with what her students could already do and needed to learn next, Chrisie prepared for instruction by asking herself these all-important questions: *What do my readers like? What do my readers do? How do my readers think?*

### What Do Readers Like?

Chrisie held informal conversations with her students and observed them talking with each other. Questions and comments like the ones that follow helped her get to know her students as readers.

- "So Maria, I see you've chosen *I'm a Frog!* (Willems 2013). What are you thinking about Elephant and Piggie? Have you read other books by Mo Willems?"

- "Marvin, you've got quite the nonfiction collection in your book box. What are you learning from these books that's interesting to you? What else would you like to read and learn about?"

- Ricky to Sarah: "Whoa, look at that bug! (*Points to illustration*) He sucks all the guts out of the caterpillar. Look, that one is coming out of its skin! Cool!"

These brief interactions revealed that Maria loved the Elephant and Piggie series because the characters are funny and she liked reading about their friendship. Marvin learned interesting information about animals and wanted to read more about dogs as well as about soccer. Ricky enjoyed non-fiction books with engaging illustrations and photographs.

Although there weren't any Mo Willems books in the guided reading collection at her school, and there may not have been any nonfiction books specifically on dogs or soccer at Marvin's level, Chrisie broadened the specifics of her students' remarks so that they applied to other books. She searched for texts that appealed to the kids in her group through the following characteristics:

- Humor

- Engaging photographs and illustrations

- Stories about friendship

- Animal- and sports-related topics

## What Do Readers Do?

As Chrisie reflected on what she saw and heard Marvin, Maria, Ricky, and Sarah do while they read, she began to see patterns emerge in their reading behaviors.

> *What do I notice about readers' stretches of accurate reading (long versus short stretches, rereading, fluency)?*
>
> Most students displayed long stretches of accuracy, reading a few sentences in a row accurately, sometimes a complete page, without having to slow down to problem-solve. Many of these stretches of accuracy were attributed to knowing a core of known high-frequency words, which propelled their reading forward and kept them from having to pause and figure out words like *then* or *went*. Accuracy ranges on level D texts and one level E text (their most recent running records) spanned from 92 to 95 percent.

*What, if anything, do readers do at the point of difficulty (stop, appeal to the teacher, check the picture, reread, make the sound of the first letters, break a word into parts)?*

Students in this group consistently checked the picture to think about what would make sense when they got to the point of difficulty and typically used a combination of meaning, structure, and beginning visual information to problem-solve (e.g., *fence/farm*). They slowed down at tricky parts but usually regained momentum quickly.

*How consistently do readers notice (monitor) when they have made an error (hesitate, stop, appeal to the teacher)? What do they do once they've noticed they've made an error (self-correct at the point of error, reread, make another attempt, read on)?*

Their most current running records showed that students monitored and self-corrected about one of every three to five errors while reading. They self-corrected errors that didn't make sense or match grammatically (e.g., *good/got*). Occasionally, when Maria and Ricky noticed something wasn't quite right and they weren't sure how to fix it, they appealed to Chrisie for help.

*How does their reading sound? To what extent do they read in meaningful phrases? Read with appropriate momentum? Use punctuation to guide their reading? Read with intonation and inflection in their voice? Apply appropriate stress on words and phrases?*

It was typical for students in this group to read in two- or three-word phrases. Sarah sometimes fell into the habit of pointing to every word as she read, making her reading sound choppy. Generally, the students in the group often neglected to use punctuation to guide their intonation and seldom conveyed characters' emotions when reading dialogue.

The patterns Chrisie observed across students led her to infer several group strengths and needs. As far as strengths were concerned, she noticed that students controlled a core of known high-frequency words, which supported accurate reading. They searched for meaning in pictures and checked their attempts against the first letter to figure out unknown words. They also consistently monitored their reading for meaning, which often resulted in the self-correction of errors.

Regarding areas of need, students' reading behaviors suggested that they would benefit from developing word-solving actions to help them look at more than just the first letter (e.g., using word parts such as -*in* or -*ook* to solve unknown words). Overall, the students needed to read in longer phrase units so that their reading would begin to sound smoother, like talking. It would also help to teach them to attend more closely to punctuation and think more about how characters feel in order to convey meaning through intonation.

### How Do Readers Think?

Chrisie reviewed anecdotal notes and thought back to conversations with her students while keeping in mind the guiding questions in Figure 2.3. The following is what Chrisie inferred about how they comprehend texts. How do Maria, Marvin, Ricky, and Sarah

*summarize the main points of what they've read?*

Maria, Marvin, and Ricky were capable of sharing key points from what they read, but often did so as these points came to mind rather than talking about stories in sequence or discussing information in categories. Sarah tended to talk less than the others, but when encouraged to say more was usually able to discuss the main points.

*predict what might happen?*

All four students were proficient at logically predicting what might happen in discussions before reading and while they read.

*connect what they know about their life, other books, and the world around them with what is happening in the text? Use these connections to deepen understanding of the text?*

The readers in this group tended to make direct connections with events and circumstances in the texts ("I went to visit the ocean, too," "Once I fell off my bike"). It was rare for them to make more sophisticated connections that helped them infer deeper meaning.

*infer meaning (feelings, motivations, themes) beyond what is explicitly stated?*

Students were adept at inferring information from pictures, especially when prompted to do so. When inferring characters' feelings and motives, they tended to stick to the basics (happy, sad) and could benefit from expanding their repertoire of ways to talk about characters. They frequently contributed to teacher-led discussions around themes (e.g., You won't know if you like something unless you try it), but were not yet initiating these types of discussions on their own.

*synthesize previously held understandings with new ones?*

When reading nonfiction texts, students frequently identified what they already knew about a topic as well as what was new or interesting to them.

*notice, use, and appreciate the author's crafting moves?*

Students in this group understood the difference between fiction and nonfiction texts and could explain how they knew a book fit in one genre or the other. They could talk about some of the author's and illustrator's basic crafting moves when Chrisie drew their attention to them, especially when discussing illustrations (e.g., facial expressions, lines to show movement). Overall, though, this wasn't an area they naturally attended to yet.

*form and share opinions about what they liked and didn't like about a text?*

These students formed basic opinions about the books they read and could sometimes support their opinions with rationales ("because she's funny," "I like bugs").

Chrisie considered the evidence she gathered to determine students' collective strengths and needs. She realized that they could predict what might happen, recall key events and details of what they read, make general connections to their lives, and form basic opinions about what they read. She needed to teach for and support summarizing narratives in order and expository texts in logical ways; using illustrations and dialogue to infer a range of emotion in characters (to support both comprehension and fluency); and engaging in more discussion about what students noticed about the book, their opinions of it, and why.

There are numerous possibilities for where we can pitch our instruction with any given group. None of them are wrong as long as they are grounded in evidence of students' interests, strengths, and needs. While we understand there are multiple options, we also recognize that we can't teach everything at once. Chrisie prioritized by asking, *What is my hunch about what will have the greatest impact on these readers at this point in time?* For these four first graders, she decided to focus on how they use punctuation, emotion, and dialogue to support phrasing and intonation. Based on evidence of how the students were thinking and talking about texts, she decided to seek out authentic opportunities to engage them in discussing how characters felt and why they felt that way, which would not only support them in thinking more deeply about characters, but also help them adjust their intonation as they read.

## Step 2: Developing Criteria for Text Selection: Text Characteristics that Support Growth

Having criteria in mind helps guide our text selection. Remember our framework for text selection:

> **IF** I have evidence that suggests [*students' interests, strengths, and needs based on their reading behaviors*] . . .

> **THEN** I'll select a book that [*characteristics of texts that will offer opportunities to build on identified strengths and support identified needs*].

Chrisie listed the evidence of strengths and needs for Maria, Marvin, Ricky, and Sarah and then determined text characteristics that would provide them with opportunities to build on their strengths and work on what they needed to become more proficient readers.

| IF I have evidence that suggests . . . | THEN I'll select a book that . . . |
|---|---|
| A need for students to expand on their descriptions of characters' feelings and elaborate on why they might feel a certain way | Has characters who experience a range of emotions or whose feelings change from the beginning to the end of the text |
| Students can make general connections and need to learn to use those connections to infer meaning | Has events or characters students can relate to |
| A need for students to learn to reflect characters' emotions through intonation | Is a narrative, includes dialogue, and has characters who express a range of emotions |
| A need for students to learn to use punctuation to guide their intonation | Uses a range of punctuation marks |

## Step 3: Determining Instructional Value: Selecting the Best Next Book

Equipped with criteria from the THEN column, Chrisie narrowed her choices of text down to two possibilities at the group's instructional level:

### Possibility 1

*The Yard Sale* by Janelle Cherrington (Scholastic 2009; level E)

*What's it about (summary)?*

Hank's grandma was moving to a new house, so he helped her sell the things she didn't want to bring with her. Many people came to the yard sale, bought Grandma's things, and reused or repurposed them. Hank surprised Grandma at the end with a present he made for her.

*What might it really be about (possible big ideas)?*

- Something old can be new again.
- Getting rid of things is easier when you see that they can go to good use.
- Family members help each other.

*Characteristics that meet the criteria:*

The text

- is a narrative that includes dialogue.
- has a few words that students may need to solve (decode) (*moving, welcome, yard, rocked, nice*).
- includes a range of punctuation and types of sentences (statements, questions, exclamatory remarks).
- explores possible big ideas that students may connect with.

*Characteristics that don't meet the criteria:*

- Characters do not experience a range of emotions that could be inferred and reflected through intonation.
- The dialogue is basic, does not vary much, and may not offer many opportunities for overt variations in intonation.

## Possibility 2

*New Boots* by Annette Smith (2000b; level E)

*What's it about (summary)?*

Mom took Jack and Billy shopping to get new rain boots. They were excited to put them on to show Dad when they got home. Mom showed the boys where to store their boots, but Billy kept his on. Later, Dad called the boys to come eat dinner, but Billy didn't come. He had fallen asleep with his boots still on.

*What might it really be about (possible big ideas or themes)?*

- Getting something new can be very exciting.
- Our actions and words show how we feel about something. (Billy must have really liked those boots!)
- Shopping can be exhausting.

*Characteristics that meet the criteria:*

The text

- has relatable content and themes (students will likely be able to relate to how it feels to get something new).
- includes characters who experience a range of emotions that is conveyed through their dialogue.
- has a range of punctuation and types of sentences (statements, questions, exclamatory remarks).
- is a narrative.
- has a few words that students may need to solve (*shouted, inside, hungry, asleep*).
- has a bit of humor to it.

*Characteristics that don't meet the criteria:*

None

Both books are high-quality texts; Maria, Marvin, Ricky, and Sarah would have likely been able to read both of them proficiently. However, given the goal of teaching for fluency with a focus on using punctuation, character emotion, and dialogue to support intonation, Chrisie decided that *New Boots* would probably be the best next book for the group. It would provide better opportunities for students to apply their learning because it met all the criteria she was looking for based on her students' interests, strengths, and needs.

The process Chrisie went through enabled her to start with what matters most—her students—then select a text that would appeal to their interests and provide opportunities to support what they do and how they think as readers. We encourage you to have a go with this same responsive process for matching readers with texts, using the IF/THEN frame as your guide (see Appendix A). As you begin to adopt this frame for thinking, you'll quickly notice the positive effect that careful text selection has on providing optimal opportunities for the learning and growth of your students.

Matching readers with books is arguably the most important step in supporting students to read with accuracy, fluency, joy, and understanding. When we start with our kids first, we have a much better chance of selecting texts that engage students' interests while offering support and manageable challenges that help us stay in our students' ever-shifting "sweet spot."

The reality is, we don't have time to complete an in-depth analysis each time we match a group of readers with a new book. In our classrooms, we balance the needs of the group with multiple facets—the books we have available, the range of reading levels in the class, the number of guided reading groups we manage. But remember, our intent here is to slow down our thinking often enough to develop habits of mind, shaping our beliefs about observing readers, selecting texts, and ultimately how we interact with and teach our students.

Not every book has to be loaded with symbolism,
irony, or musical language . . . but it seems
to me that every book—at least every one
worth reading—is about something.

—STEPHEN KING (2001)

# CHAPTER
# 3

## Considering Meaning:
# WHAT'S IT ABOUT?
# WHAT MIGHT IT REALLY
# BE ABOUT?

On December 11, 2014, David Greene and author Ann Patchett introduced a book to adults for National Public Radio's first *Morning Edition Book Club*:

> **PATCHETT:** *It's called* Deep Down Dark: The Untold Stories of 33 Men Buried in a Chilean Mine, and the Miracle That Set Them Free—*it's a heck of a subtitle . . . by Hector Tobar.*

> **GREENE:** *You almost know exactly what the book is about from the title itself, but this is going back to 2010—these thirty-three miners who were trapped 2,000 feet underground in a mine in Chile for sixty-nine days, which is astounding. Tell us a little more about the book and why you think this would be a good read for us.*

> **PATCHETT:** *I love this book . . . It's a riveting story. It was riveting when we were watching it on the news. It's riveting in the book. You want to make sure these men are safe. Even though we already know they're safe, there's an enormous amount of suspense and tension—how they're going to get through this.*

Later in the discussion, Patchett sets us up for deeper reading by providing big questions to grapple with as we read *Deep Down Dark*.

PATCHETT: *Hector Tobar's writing, which is so beautiful and so thoughtful that he's taking on all of the big issues of life. You know, what is life worth? What is the value of one human life? What is faith? Who do we become in our darkest hour?*

As we craft introductions for readers, regardless of whether they are kindergartners or adults, our goal is to invite and guide them to *use* meaning to develop a rich understanding on their own, just as Patchett's captivating questions spark ideas for us to consider as we read *Deep Down Dark*.

Once we've taken the time to carefully match our readers with texts, we're ready to start planning how to introduce those books to students in the guided reading group. As you review the following four steps for crafting an effective book introduction, notice that this process begins by acknowledging that meaning is at the heart of reading.

| |
|---|
| 1. Read the book for meaning. Think about what it's about and what it might really be about. Craft a meaning statement and a launching statement. |
| 2. Analyze how the book works (organizational structure and features). Plan how to support students (if necessary). |
| 3. Identify potentially challenging language structures and plan how to support students with them (if necessary). |
| 4. Determine words that may be difficult to solve (recognize or decode), or to understand (vocabulary), and plan how to support students with them (if necessary). |

As we dive into the first step throughout this chapter, we will introduce these procedures and thinking processes to plan meaning-driven book introductions:

- analyzing texts to consider what they are about (literal level) and what they *might really* be about (deeper themes and ideas),

- crafting a meaning statement that sets up the reader to think about the meaning of the whole text,

- actively engaging students in meaning-making during the book introduction, and

- crafting a launching statement that sends students off to begin their reading with meaning at the forefront of their minds.

We break down each of these procedures in detail, with the goal that, with practice, they will become habits of mind that guide how you plan book introductions.

## ANALYZING A TEXT FOR MEANING: WHAT'S IT ABOUT?

In Patchett and Greene's exchange, we are drawn to consider both the literal and deeper levels of the book. The literal, by recounting some of the events of this astounding story, and the deeper, by exploring the bigger meanings of life, intrigue us enough to want to pick up the book and read it. Similarly, we aim to tap into both literal and deeper levels of meaning as a way of intriguing our students. To prepare enticing introductions, we get to know the text well ourselves, beginning with the literal level. One of the first questions we ask ourselves, *What's the book about?*, gives us a sense of the plot (narrative) or of important information (expository text).

### Analyzing Narratives

Something we all do, probably quickly, as we peruse books for children, is notice what's happening in the story and summarize the plot. We analyze the progression of the story as well as the characters that are important to it. At this level of analysis, it is important to notice which character you are attending to, as it may affect how you introduce the story. It often makes sense to introduce the story through the main character's eyes, but when stories have more than one main character, our suggestion is to decide which one students will connect with most easily.

Recently, Kath and our colleague Charlene O'Brien were analyzing guided reading books with a group of teachers. They realized that with books featuring parents and children, their tendency was to introduce the text from the parents' perspective. In the text *Bedtime* (Smith 2000d), for example, teachers quickly connected with Mom, who was trying to get her son Jack to go to bed. Their initial introduction started like this: "It is bedtime, and Jack's mother is trying really hard to get him to stop playing and go to bed." Then they listened to a group of kindergartners read the text and realized how focused the readers were on the younger brother, Billy, who was already in bed waiting for his bedtime story. The impromptu comments from children included "Billy wants to read the book," "Jack's not listening," and "Billy's in bed!" The kids were attending mostly to characters their own age.

The teachers decided a better introduction might have started like this: "It's bedtime and Jack is having such a great time playing that he doesn't want to stop! Look at Billy, though. Billy knows that Mom will read him a story once he's in bed. I wonder what Jack will think about this." Both meaning statements support students in thinking about what's happening in the story, but we learned that day to introduce the story from the lens of a character whom the kids—not necessarily the adults—might identify with most. When the teachers applied this understanding to text introductions for subsequent lessons, they found that students engaged more because the teachers set them up to think about the story in ways that were more relevant to them.

## Analyzing Expository Texts

We think about the topics and subtopics when we read expository texts. Our answer to the question "What's it about?" often lies in the important information the author conveys about these topics and subtopics. For example, the book *Big Ships Need Tugboats* (Woolley 2009) could be summarized by expressing the main idea: "This book is about all the ways tugboats help big ships leave and return to docks." Or, the summary could be expanded to include a bit more about the subtopics: "This book is about the ways tugboats help big ships. It tells how tugboats help big ships stop, get close to the dock, and leave the dock safely. It also tells us how tugboats prevent big ships from running into things."

## Tapping into What Level A and B Books Are About

A primary purpose of emergent leveled texts (A and B) is to provide opportunities for students to learn how to control early reading behaviors, some of which include directionality (turning pages from front to back, reading from left to right and top to bottom), matching voice with print (one-to-one correspondence), recognizing and using familiar words to monitor and propel reading, and searching pictures for meaning or using the initial letter to make an attempt at an unknown word. These simple stories follow a pattern, enabling students to hold on to the sentence structure with ease while noticing the white space between each word to help them point and match their spoken words to the words on the page. At levels A, B, and sometimes C, there isn't usually much of a plot on which to build a summary.

At first glance, many level A and B texts seem to merely consist of captions for individual pictures ("I like _____," "Dad can _____"), but when you look a little closer, there are often possible lines of thinking or themes that tie the pages together. Beverley Randell, author of numerous Rigby PM readers, explains: "My aim has never varied. I believe that books used for learning to read should have the same qualities as good picture story books, and should be shaped to bring children success, not failure; enjoyment, not boredom; and understanding, not bewilderment" (2000, 31). Her words—"shaped to bring children success . . . enjoyment . . . and understanding"—remind us that the authors of these books, regardless of the level, write with meaning in mind. It's our job as teachers to tap into possible meanings and bring them to the forefront of our students' thinking so that they come to expect meaning-making from every book they read.

We can support emergent-level readers with meaning by creating backstories for the texts we introduce to them. One way to do this is to focus on a specific character (if there is one). Try to think of what the character might have been doing before or after the story takes place, what he or she thinks, or what he or she wants. For example, *The Toy Box* (Smith, Giles, and Randell 2000) shows a little girl putting toys into a toy box. On the left side of each two-page spread is the text and a little picture of a type of toy (e.g., trucks). The right side of the page shows the girl sitting with a pile of toys and putting the toy from the facing page into her toy box. The second word in each sentence is the only one that changes on each page ("The _____ are in the box"). At first glance, the book may be taken as just a list of toys that are in the box; however, a backstory can layer in more meaning. We might introduce it by saying, "It was a rainy day and this little girl played with all of her toys. She made a mess, but she knows how important it is to put things away when she is finished with them. Look at how careful she is when she puts her toys in her toy box. On each page she shows us which toy she is putting in the box. Let's take a look at all the toys. . . ."

Another way to create a backstory is to think about a character who might be suggested but is missing from the book. As an example, consider *The Farm* by Mary Fried (1996), a level A book. The sentences are simple and written on the left page (e.g., "Here is the pig . . ."). A picture of the animal and text of the sound it makes appear on the right page. There are no humans pictured in this story, but we can infer that a farmer is around to take care of the animals. We might begin introducing the story by saying, "When the animals on the farm wake up, they make lots of noise to let the farmer know they are hungry. Let's see which animals are ready for breakfast." Adding a brief backstory to this list book helps connect the pages with the idea that the farmer is noticing which animals need to eat. It also gives the kids something meatier to discuss after reading (no pun intended!).

Regardless of the level, this first step of analyzing what a text is about isn't enough by itself. We want our readers to think deeply about the books they read. Therefore, we push ourselves to also consider what the book *might really* be about; we search for what the deeper meaning, themes, or big ideas may be.

## ANALYZING A TEXT FOR MEANING: WHAT MIGHT IT REALLY BE ABOUT?

Proficient readers expect to uncover deeper layers of meaning in complex texts, but we sometimes stop short of envisioning possible deeper layers of meaning in the seemingly simplistic books we introduce to our students. Guess what? They aren't simplistic to kids! The popularity of guided reading over the past few decades has brought with it a surge in high-quality leveled texts that touch on many themes that kids either grapple with in their everyday lives or are interested in learning more about (e.g., Why do I look different? Who are my true friends? When can I make decisions for myself?). We argue that most well-written books, even at the earliest levels, have deeper layers of meaning that the author and illustrator intended to be considered by the reader. Supporting this theory is Beverley Randell. "We know that in every story we are trying to make contact with the minds of small children," she writes. "Meaning affects the choice of every subject, meaning is the thread of logic that runs through every story, meaning shapes every page, every paragraph, every sentence, and every illustration" (2000, 10). Reading should always be about understanding, even for those who are just beginning to learn how to solve words, how to check on themselves, and how to infer characters' feelings or thoughts. We owe it to our students to prepare for the introduction by considering the themes in books and nudging them toward discovering big ideas about things that matter to them. Helping students establish the readerly habit of developing ideas right from the start and considering *what they think* of those ideas sets them up to be lifelong critical thinkers about text (and movies and topics and situations).

Our first step in supporting students with exploring big ideas and compelling questions is to understand the text deeply, beyond the plot, as authentic readers ourselves. This habit of mind requires us to ask the question, *What* might *it* really *be about?* There are two keywords in this question: *really* gets at the big idea, and *might* allows for multiple interpretations.

It's important to reiterate that we aren't seeking a single specific meaning for a text. In asking, "What *might* this book *really* be about?" we remain open to multiple interpretations, knowing that the goal is not for students to come away with *our* interpretation of the text, but rather to freely interpret (and support) their own ideas while remaining open to the ideas of others. The more you consider what a book *might really* be about and explore possibilities with colleagues, the more you'll find common themes emerge. Teachers often choose a prominent idea to tie into the introduction, but if we make it a practice to consider multiple themes, it is easier to change course in the event that students take the conversation in another direction.

The question "What *might* this book *really* be about?" may seem somewhat simplistic, but the answer may not come so readily to those who are not in the habit of thinking about the underlying meaning of texts. Chrisie's mentor, Tina Henry, took teachers through a process of text analysis that we borrow from throughout this chapter. This process helps us guide students toward reading for the meaning of the whole text (the top line of the hierarchy that we first introduced in Chapter 1). In our experience, slowing down the planning process and routinely exploring the questions *What's it about?* and *What* might *it* really *be about?* becomes a habit of mind that gets easier with practice once you start to recognize common themes in books.

Below we share two processes to analyze what a text might really be about: considering a main character and determining the gist or topic of the text.

1. **Consider a main character, then state a generalizable theme**. <u>Pay attention to characters' desires or problems and resolutions, relationships, changes, motives, and lessons learned. Ask yourself:</u>

   - *What did the character want?* or *What was the character's problem?* In *Bedtime* (Smith 2000a), Jack wanted to keep playing with his new red car.

- *How did the character get what he or she wanted, solve the problem, or change?* Jack finally went to bed. The text doesn't explicitly tell us why he went to bed; we have to infer. It could have been because his mother was telling him to go to bed. Or it could have been because he saw that Billy, his younger brother, was already in bed and he didn't want to be shown up. Or it could have been that he didn't want to miss out on hearing a bedtime story.

- *What did the character learn (if anything)?* Jack may have learned that while playing with toys is fun, bedtime can be fun, too, because you get to listen to a story. Or, he may have learned that sometimes it is hard to stop doing something fun, even when there is something else that is important to do.

State as a generalizable theme. Think about how the characters' experiences might be generalized to reflect universal experiences that students can connect to and apply to other stories or situations in life. For *Bedtime,* one possibility might be, "There are some routines in life that we just have to do, even when we don't really want to do them."

Another way to analyze texts for big ideas is to first determine the gist of the text. This works with both narrative and expository texts.

2.  **Determine the gist or topic of the text, then state it as a generalizable theme.** It can be challenging to determine the theme of some books. One way to do so is to begin by summing up the book in one or two words, identifying the gist of it. Once you note the gist of the book, you can more easily get to the message. Many books have similar topics, so we provide a few categories to get you started in your thinking about them in Figures 3.1 and 3.2. Keep in mind that the categories we suggest are merely a starting place. You'll discover many more as you apply this process with books you select.

Figure 3.1
FICTION CATEGORIES TO GUIDE DISCOVERY OF THE GIST

| Experiences | Values | Relationships | Learning About Yourself |
|---|---|---|---|
| Trying something new | Responsibility | Trust | Getting in trouble |
| Overcoming fears | Sharing | Friendship | Making decisions |
| Celebrations/ milestones | Rules (following/ breaking) | Family | Imagination |
| Home/school/ vacation | Mistakes (moving past/admitting/ forgiving) | Getting along | Emotions/ self-control (disappointment, patience, excitement, jealousy, etc.) |
| Adventures | Fairness | Dealing with difficult people | |
| Getting hurt/having accidents/making mistakes | | Cooperation | |
| | | Helping others | Growing and changing |
| Humorous situations | | Judging others | |

Figure 3.2
NONFICTION CATEGORIES TO GUIDE DISCOVERY OF THE GIST

| Nature | Relationships | Concepts |
|---|---|---|
| Life cycles | Family | Exploration |
| Survival | Friends | Change |
| Weather | Teamwork | Interdependence |
| Space | Community | Perspective |
| Habitats | | Function |
| | | Form |
| | | Adaptations |
| | | Comparisons |

<u>Sum up the book in one or two words</u>. For example, the gist of *Bedtime* (described on the previous page) might be "responsibility" or "following rules." As another example, *Is This a Monster?* (Lovell andSnowball 1995) is a book with

photographs that zoom in on a specific part of an animal. One page shows an unrecognizable close-up and the next page shows the entire animal. The gist of this book might be "unique bodies."

<u>State the gist as a generalizable theme</u>. As with the narrative process, here we take the gist or topic and make it universal so that students see the links between concepts and experiences. To craft this statement, we might answer one of the following questions: *What does this text say about the gist or topic?* or *What might the author want readers to think about this topic?*

Answering these questions in a sentence or two should expand the gist into a theme. When asking, *What might the author want readers to think about 'responsibility' in* Bedtime*?* we arrive at the same theme suggested previously: "There are some routines in life that we just have to do, even when we don't really want to do them." When asking, *What might the author want us to think about 'unique bodies'?* in *Is This a Monster?*, we might respond, "Living things have features that make them unique" or "Sometimes when you look at a part of something, it seems scary or strange, but when you zoom out, you see how it fits in with the whole." Further examples of moving from gist to big ideas are provided in Figures 3.3 and 3.4.

Figure 3.3

FICTION EXAMPLES: MOVING FROM GIST TO BIG IDEAS

| Title | Sum up the book in one or two words.— Gist: | Big Idea:<br>What does this text say about the gist or topic?<br>What might the author want readers to think about this topic? |
|---|---|---|
| *Come On, Tim* (Giles 2006) | Overcoming fears | You feel proud of yourself when you try something that seems scary.<br>Other people can help you overcome your fears.<br>Once you give something a chance, you often realize it isn't as scary as it first seemed. |

*(continues)*

*(continued )*

| | | |
|---|---|---|
| *Father Bear Goes Fishing* (Randell 2006) | Responsibility | We take care of those who depend on us. |
| *The Gym Teacher from the Black Lagoon* (Thaler 1994) | Judging others | You shouldn't judge others before you get to know them. Don't always believe what others say about people. |

Figure 3.4

NONFICTION EXAMPLES: MOVING FROM GIST TO BIG IDEAS

| Title | Sum up the book in one or two words.— Gist: | Big Idea: What does this text say about the gist or topic? What might the author want readers to think about this topic? |
|---|---|---|
| *Garbage to Garden* (Lawrence 2015) | Composting/ recycling | Some food parts that we would normally throw away can have an important use in creating new foods and flowers in gardens. |
| *Our Clothes* (Wilson and Davis 2001) | Needs | Clothes have many purposes. They keep us safe, help us have fun, and help us look nice. |
| *Surprising Sharks* (Davies 2005) | Perspective | Sharks have a bad reputation for threatening humans, but it is humans who kill more sharks. |
| *Where Does Your Pizza Come From?* (Dufresne 2015c) | Food sources | There are many steps to food production. We may not be aware of many jobs that are related to the food we eat. |

## A Note on the Importance of Illustrations

Illustrations, especially in early leveled text, help us construct the plot, identify subplots, and determine the big ideas of stories. Take the book *At the Ocean* (Dufresne 2007), for example. The text alone is simple, with each page offering some variation of *"Come in the water, Dad!"* or *"No," said Dad.* Page after page, the two teenage sons beg their dad to come in the water, yet he stays at the shoreline saying no. On the last page of the text, Dad is actually in the water, soaking wet. Did he finally decide to go in the water? If so, why? If not, what happened? Taking a close look at the setting, and bearing in mind that Dad says "Oh, no!" on the last page, we might introduce the book by drawing students' attention to the waves on the last two pages of the book. We discuss what is happening with the waves and whether we think a big wave got closer to the shoreline and got Dad all wet or Dad went in the water to make his sons happy. If you take the first perspective, the gist of this story might be "surprise" and the big idea might be "Sometimes we are surprised by nature." If you take the second perspective, the gist might be "giving in" and the message might be "Sometimes we put others' happiness before our own." Readers might discuss what the boys or Dad were thinking on this last page. Did Dad want to go in but the water was too cold? Too rough? Did he go in to make his kids happy? Why did the kids want Dad to come in the water? These conversations lead to higher-level thinking—inferring characters' thoughts and motivations—rather than simply discussing the events that occurred.

## Considering Various Perspectives: Tapping into What Matters to Kids

Allow us to take a brief detour as we return to the importance of analyzing texts from our students' perspectives. We know this book is about book introductions for guided reading, but we are going take a quick drive down Read-Aloud Road for a moment to illustrate the importance of considering big ideas that matter to students.

At a recent professional development session, a group of literacy coaches reread the text *Chrysanthemum* by Kevin Henkes (1991) before watching a video of an interactive read-aloud with a kindergarten class. This story is about a little mouse girl, Chrysanthemum, who loves her unique name and is excited about starting school. On the first day, some classmates tease her about her name. That evening, her parents comfort her and try to reassure her about how special her name is. The teasing continues until a beloved music teacher tells the class that she has a similarly unusual name, Delphinium Twinkle, and suddenly the classmates want to change their names to those of flowers as well. When the facilitator of the professional development suggested that the coaches think about the big ideas of the book, they shared a few thoughts ("It is okay to be different," "Be proud of your uniqueness").

After watching the video, the coaches analyzed students' responses. Students' spontaneous comments during the read-aloud included "She is sad now," "She just wants to be their friend," "They were making fun of her name," "She's saying mean things," "Say, '*Don't do that again!*'" "The big girl is being bad to her," and "Tell them to stop." Though the kindergartners focused on a different angle than the coaches did, the student comments illustrate for us what they understood about what the story *might really* be about. The bigger ideas the children came up with were about being teased (and what to do about it), wanting to fit in (and how it feels when you don't), and friendship (and what to do when it's hard to make friends). Their ideas didn't precisely match the big ideas the coaches came up with, but they were directly tied to the text and were evidence that the students understood beyond the plot level. Five- and six-year-olds can think beyond the literal level of summarizing what happened in the book. In this case, they related to how vulnerable it feels to navigate friendships. Chrysanthemum liked her name but was willing to change it to fit in with the rest of the class. Sometimes kids are mean. Sometimes we get teased. Sometimes we tease other kids. Sometimes our feelings are hurt. Sometimes we hurt someone's feelings. Sometimes we feel bad about what we have said or done. These feelings and what to do in response to them are real-life big ideas that kids want and need to explore. And books, regardless of whether they are read to or by children, can help them do just that.

These kindergartners were on their way to challenging ideas and conclusions as they talked back to the text and talked with their classmates about why Chrysanthemum didn't tell Rita and Jo to stop, and what they might have done in that situation. This thinking work was enabled because their teacher followed their lead and didn't remain rigid in trying to guide them to "get" or say what she originally considered to be the theme. Investing the time to know the book well allowed the teacher to take a tentative stance; she realized that her students' perspectives were also supported by the text and constituted big ideas that were relatable and meaningful to them.

Once we determine what the book is about and what it *might really* be about and consider what our students' perspectives might be, we can begin to craft an introduction in a way that prepares kids to construct some of these understandings for themselves. The next section addresses how one very tiny slice of a child's day—the book introduction in guided reading—has the power to support students as they explore big ideas and compelling questions.

## Moving from Text Analysis to Planning the Introduction

Maria Nichols, one of our favorite authors on comprehension, writes:

> *We must have a sense of the rich meaning we hope the children will build. With fiction text, this means not only knowing the literal story, but developing our own understanding of the heart of the story (big idea or theme). Complex text may encompass more than one theme, so flexibility and an awareness of the options is crucial. Then, we must plan ways of supporting the children in drawing on the heart of the story as they consider their own interactions with the real world. (2006, 55)*

In introducing texts to students, we can begin to "plan ways of supporting the children in drawing on the heart of the story" by beginning with a meaning statement.

## CONSTRUCTING A MEANING STATEMENT

A meaning statement is often the first part of the book introduction, usually one to three sentences that provide a short summary by introducing characters and setting up the plot or giving an overview of the book's topics. The meaning statement can be likened to the blurb on the back of paperback books ("This story is about . . . ," "In this book . . ."). When we craft the meaning statement by pulling from what we've summarized ("What's the book about?") and what we've determined to be a big idea ("What *might* the book *really* be about?"), the readers comprehend the text more effectively. Alternatively, the meaning statement may sound more natural if it consists mostly of the summary and is followed by a launching statement that prompts students to think about what the book *might really* be about.

Now that we have several processes for considering what books are about and what they *might really* be about, we can move on to this next step of crafting the meaning statement. To review, the steps are as follows:

1. Summarize the plot (narrative) or information/topics (expository) in one or two sentences. ("What's the book about?")

2. Consider the possible big ideas. ("What *might* the book *really* be about?")

3. Craft a meaning statement that ties the summary and the big ideas together. Or, use a variation of the summary as the meaning statement and the big ideas for the launching statement.

Notice, below, how we use these steps to craft a meaning statement for *Come On, Tim* (Giles 2006), which we analyzed earlier in Figure 3.3.

### Step 1. Summarize the plot or information/topics in a few sentences.

Tim sees his friends climb to the top of the fort and slide down the pole. He wants to slide down too, but is scared to try. Tim's friends and teacher encourage him, and he safely makes it down the pole.

### Step 2. Consider what the book *might really* be about.

The gist is overcoming fears. Possible big ideas include "You feel proud of yourself when you try something that seems scary," "Other people can help you overcome your fears," or "Once you give something a chance, you often realize it isn't as scary as it first seemed."

### Step 3. Craft a meaning statement that ties the first two steps together.

In *Come On, Tim,* Tim sees his friends Michael and Anna climb up the fort and go down the pole. He wants to do it too, but once he gets to the top, he gets scared to go down. He's going to have to be brave to overcome his fear.

**An alternative meaning statement:** Tim watches his friends Michael and Anna climb up to the top of the fort and slide down the pole. He wants to do it too, but is scared to slide down. We'll read what happens as his friends and teacher, Ms. Hill, encourage him to go down.

**Launching statement (at the end of the introduction):** As you read, think about how Tim might be feeling at different parts of the story and why he's feeling that way.

Here's another example using this thinking process to construct a meaning statement for *Where Does Your Pizza Come From?* (Dufresne 2015c), which we mentioned previously in Figure 3.4.

### Step 1. Summarize the plot or information/topics in a few sentences.

This book lists several important ingredients for making pizza. It shows where each ingredient comes from or how it is made.

### Step 2. Consider what the book *might really* be about.

Big ideas might include "There are many steps to food production" or "We may not be aware of many jobs that are related to the food we eat."

### Step 3. Craft a meaning statement that ties the first two steps together.

It's amazing to realize how many types of jobs there are in the world. Although this book isn't exactly about jobs, it is about where the ingredients for pizza come from—the tomatoes, the flour, the cheese—and makes us think about all the work that goes into creating each ingredient long before the pizza is made!

We've broken these steps down to illustrate the process. Very often, as you are analyzing a text for the plot or important details, you recognize a few bigger ideas and immediately incorporate them into a meaning statement. With practice, you'll find that these steps will become second nature as you plan meaning statements that help students read for the meaning of the whole text.

## STUDENT ENGAGEMENT AND MEANING-MAKING

In guided reading, students should be physically and mentally engaged with the text; they should be noticing, thinking, talking, and listening the moment the introduction begins. Once we've drawn students in with a brief overview of what the book will be about, we give them a chance to dip into the text, making sure they each have a copy of the book in their hands. Some teachers hold the book while giving the meaning statement and then pass a copy of the text to each child. Others pass out the texts while giving the overview. The point is to encourage active engagement from the start. The sooner the text is in students' hands, the better, as students continue to construct meaning by turning pages, thinking, and talking. All this will help them when they begin to read.

As we turn to a few key pages during the introduction, we draw students' attention to important plot points, information, or illustrations and invite them to share what they think. We invite them to predict, search for more information, or infer. We encourage them to engage with each other and build on one another's thinking. We may also layer in key vocabulary or phrases and pose ideas for students to consider.

When posing ideas, we suggest using a combination of open-ended questions and statements, especially those that are related to the big idea of the book or help students tap into their related experiences. We have been experimenting with making statements instead of always asking questions. For example, if reading *Father Bear Goes Fishing* (Randell 2006), instead of "How long do you think Father Bear took to catch those fish?" try "I wonder how long it took Father Bear to get all those fish." You might even rephrase something that is happening on a page (e.g., "Father Bear took a long time") and wait for the kids to respond. It may not happen the first time. You may need to model a bit. The more teachers are authentic participants in the introduction (as opposed to interrogators eliciting specific responses), the more actively engaged students will be.

## CRAFTING A LAUNCHING STATEMENT: KEEPING MEANING AT THE FOREFRONT

The launch, the final component of the book introduction, leaves students thinking about the whole book, or an aspect of meaning, just before beginning to read. The launch is often closely tied to the meaning statement and gives students an idea of what they might think about or consider as they read. Though it comes at the end of the introduction (see Figure 3.5), we include it in this chapter because it is so closely tied to crafting the meaning statement. During an actual book introduction, students will engage in discussion after the meaning statement, explore some of the text, and may attend to the overall text structure (Chapter 4), rehearse a few language structures (Chapter 5), or attend to a few words (Chapter 6) if necessary. We cover a lot of ground in our brief introductions, and since we want meaning to be the primary thing children consider when reading, it is helpful to bring them back to meaning just before sending them off to read their books.

Figure 3.5
STRUCTURE OF A BOOK INTRODUCTION

Overall Meaning Statement

Support with Challenging Characteristics
(when necessary)

- Text Structures

- Language Structures

- Words

- Other Features

Launching Statement/Question

Launching statements often begin with an invitational phrase such as "As you read . . ." or "When you read today. . . ." How we complete the sentence can have a great effect on what students attend to and what they see as the purpose of reading, so we consider our word choice carefully and keep our emphasis on meaning-making as often as possible. To illustrate, Figure 3.6 shows some possible launches for *Father Bear Goes Fishing* (Randell 2006) along with what they may imply the purpose for reading is.

Figure 3.6

LAUNCHING STATEMENTS AND IMPLIED PURPOSES FOR *FATHER BEAR GOES FISHING*

| Launching Statement | Implied Purpose for Reading |
| --- | --- |
| When you read today, notice one or two words that are hard and write them down on your sticky note. We'll talk about them when you finish reading. | Focus on the words. If you don't know a word, divert your attention from the text and write it down, then keep reading until you come to another word you don't know and do the same. I will tell you what the word means when you are done. |
| If you get stuck on tricky words as you read, look for parts you know to figure them out. | Read this book for the purpose of applying a strategy for word-solving. |
| Read to see if Father Bear ever catches any fish. | Read to find out how the story ends. |
| As you read, think about how Mother Bear and Baby Bear feel while Father Bear is fishing. | Focus on the characters and their feelings. This is where the heart of the story is. |
| As you read, think about how much work it took Father Bear to get all those fish. | This is also the heart of the story, but from Father Bear's perspective. |

As you can see, the way we send students off to begin reading implies certain messages about their job as readers, which in turn shape their theories of reading. Since we want students to be meaning-makers, we try to send them off with statements that are tied to aspects of what the book is about or what it *might really* be about, replicating the same purposes that we as proficient readers follow to see how the story unfolds and to consider the heart and big ideas of it.

With all of this in mind, reflect on how the launching statements in the last two rows of Figure 3.6 accomplish this goal. We have found that adding the phrase *think about* helps to keep the focus on thinking and meaning-making. Some possibilities for students to consider while reading might include the following:

- Think about how [character] changes from the beginning to the end of the book.

- As you read, think about how [two characters] are getting along.

- Think about how you might react if you were in a similar situation.

- Think about how the character overcomes his or her challenge.

- When you read today, think about what happens at the end and how it compares with what you expected.

- Think about what the author might be trying to tell us about [topic, concept, theme].

- While reading, think about what you learn that is interesting to you.

- Think about how your understanding of [topic/concept] has deepened.

- Think about how your ideas are confirmed or are changing.

These launching statements often anchor our conversation about the book after students have finished reading (Chapter 7). In fact, an alternative way to plan for the launch might be to consider points you want to discuss with students and then work backward to craft a launching statement that will nudge their awareness and thinking in that direction.

## PULLING IT ALL TOGETHER

Now that we've explored a process for planning for the meaning and launching statement portions of the book introduction, let's follow second-grade teacher Michelle Holtzclaw as she plans to introduce *The Fox Who Cried "Help!"* (Staman 2008) to a group of her students. Below, you'll find both her thinking as she planned for the lesson as well as the notes she recorded on her planning sheet (Figure 3.7; a blank copy of this sheet can be found in Appendix B). Then, we'll look at how her intentional planning began to affect students' thinking about the book even before they read the first word.

## Summarize the plot (narrative) or information/topics (expository) in one or two sentences.
## (What's the book about?)

Little Fox got bored while he was outside playing and decided to play a trick on Father Fox and Mother Fox by making them think he got hurt. Despite getting in trouble the first time he did it, he played the trick again. Then, when he really did get hurt and cried for help, Mother and Father didn't believe him.

## Consider the possible big ideas.
## (What might the book really be about?)

If you make a habit of lying, no one will believe you, even when you tell the truth.

## Craft a meaning statement.

In this story, Little Fox gets bored while playing outside and decides to play a trick on his parents. He pretends to get hurt when he's not, and his parents don't like that he lied to them. Then, when Little Fox really does get hurt, they don't believe him and don't come out to help.

## Craft a launching statement that sends students into their reading with something to think about.

As you read this book, think about what Little Fox might learn about playing a trick on others.

Figure 3.7
PLANNING SHEET FOR *THE FOX WHO CRIED "HELP!"*

**Group/Students:** Camryn, Luna, Fabio, Marco          **Date:** _____

**Running Record Student:** Camryn   **Running Record Book/Level:** Little Red Riding Hood/ I

**New Book/Level:** The Fox Who Cried "Help!"/ I

**Introducing the Text:**

*Meaning Statement:*
In this story, Little Fox gets bored while playing outside and decides to play a trick on his parents. He pretends to get hurt when he's not, and his parents don't like that he lied to them. Then, when Little Fox really does get hurt, they don't believe him and don't come out to help.

*Support (how book works, language structure, words):*

p. 3 float phrase "down on the ground"

pp. 4, 5- angry—rehearse like Father Fox would say it, "Don't do that . . .," locate laughed

*Launch:*

As you read this book, think about what Little Fox might learn about lying to others.

**Anecdotal Notes:**

| Student: Camryn | Student: Marco | Student: Fabio |
|---|---|---|
| | | |
| Student: Luna | Student: | Student: |
| | | |

**Text Discussion:**
Talk about what you think Little Fox might have learned.

**Group Teaching Point:**
Looking through the word to solve or self-correct, or reading with intonation.

**Word Work:**
Change a word by adding -ed to show it happened in the past.

| MS. HOLTZCLAW | This book is called *The Fox Who Cried "Help!"* |
| CAMRYN | *The Fox Who Cried "Help!"*? I thought it was *The Boy Who Cried "Wolf!"* |
| LUNA | Why is it *cried* help? |
| MS. HOLTZCLAW | It's like shouted or said, sometimes you cry out—"Help!" You say it loud. |
| CAMRYN | I only know the story *The Boy Who Cried "Wolf!"* I didn't know there was one called *The Fox Who Cried "Help!"* |
| MS. HOLTZCLAW | *The Fox Who Cried "Help!"*—well, we'll have to see if there are some similarities to the book you know. In this story, Little Fox gets bored playing outside and decides to play a trick on his parents. He pretends to get hurt when he's not, and his parents don't like it. Then, when he really gets hurt, they don't come out to help him. |
| FABIO | Why? |
| MARCO | He's lying. |
| MS. HOLTZCLAW | We'll have to read and see (*passes books out to students*). Let's take a look at a few things together. Turn to page 3. Look at that picture of Little Fox. Can you tell what he's saying? "Help!" He got down on the ground to pretend that he was hurt. |
| LUNA | Oh, he's acting it. |
| MARCO | He's *lying*. |
| MS. HOLTZCLAW | Yeah, he's acting hurt even though he's not. Turn the page. Look at the picture—at Little Fox and Father Fox. |
| LUNA | Oh, he was angry. |
| MS. HOLTZCLAW | How can you tell Father's angry? |
| FABIO | Look at his eyes and his mouth. |
| MS. HOLTZCLAW | Yeah, his expression. And look at something else (*points to Father Fox wagging his finger at Little Fox*). Have you ever had your parents do that to you when you're in trouble for something? |
| CAMRYN | Yeah, actually my parents do that a lot of times to me. |
| FABIO | Mine too. |
| MS. HOLTZCLAW | Well, what happened was, Mother and Father Fox were inside and they heard Little Fox crying "Help!" and Father Fox came out there and—look at Little Fox. |

| FABIO | He's happy. |
|---|---|
| MS. HOLTZCLAW | Yeah, he's smiling, and look (*pointing to the text*), he said, "'Ha, ha!' laughed Little Fox." Find where it says *laughed* and run your finger under it. (*Students locate, say, and run their finger under the word.*) It sounds like there'd be an *f* in the middle but it's actually *gh*. So "'Ha, Ha!', laughed Little Fox." He thought it was fun to play a trick on them. But we know Father Fox didn't think it was funny. He said, "Don't do that again." How do you think he'd say it? |
| CAMRYN | (*Wagging her finger, using an angry voice*) "Don't do that again!" |
| MS. HOLTZCLAW | Yeah, with an expression like he's mad. All of you try it the way Father Fox would say it—angry. |
| STUDENTS | (*Angrily*) "Don't do that again!" |
| MS. HOLTZCLAW | Now, turn to page 9. |
| CAMRYN | Now he's not as happy anymore. |
| FABIO | Now Mother Fox is out there with him. |
| LUNA | She's not happy at all. I think the mother fox is worse than the father. |
| MS. HOLTZCLAW | Notice who's not out there. Father Fox thinks Little Fox is playing a trick again, but Mother Fox thinks, "Oh, well, maybe he's really hurt. I need to go outside and check," but she doesn't look very happy. |
| LUNA | I think the mother fox is worser than the father. She looks more angry. |
| MS. HOLTZCLAW | Yeah, so angry that when she goes back inside and Little Fox cries for help again, she and Father Fox ignore him. The trouble is, Little Fox really is hurt this time. Let's go ahead and read, and as you read, think about the lesson Little Fox may have learned from doing all this. |
| MARCO | Tell the truth. |
| MS. HOLTZCLAW | Maybe. Go ahead and read and then we'll talk about what you all think when you finish. |

In the four and a half minutes it took Michelle to introduce the book, she was able to provide students with an overview of what the book was about, nudge them toward thinking about what it might really be about, share the character's motive (he was bored), engage students in discussion of characters' feelings, plant some of the language of the text (*got down on the ground*), define vocabulary (*cried*), and draw attention to a word that may have been challenging for students to solve on their own (*laughed*). Each of these intentional teaching moves freed students to focus on the greater meaning of the text as they read and enabled them to discuss the characters, themes, and comparisons to *The Boy Who Cried Wolf* when they finished. More importantly, the book introduction set students up for a very enjoyable interaction with a book that they loved.

Although kids read the text themselves in guided reading, there is a certain level of responsibility that still belongs to us as the teachers. We choose and analyze the book, craft an introduction, determine teaching points, and guide discussions. In doing all of this, we strive to balance the amount of support we provide with opportunities for students to construct and extend the meaning of texts.

We sometimes hear teachers hesitate to give rich book introductions for fear of giving the meaning away or providing too much support for the readers. Our goal in teaching is to consistently shift responsibility over to students. While we work on doing this, however, we mustn't confuse guided reading with independent reading. In guided reading, we introduce books at students' instructional level and therefore must provide some support.

Perhaps it's helpful to recognize that even proficient readers almost always enter a text with some knowledge of what it's going to be about and what it *might really* be about. Think about yourself as a reader for a moment. When you walk into a bookstore to pick out a new book, we doubt that you select one based on the front cover and title alone. Instead, you open it up, read the blurb on the inside cover, and likely flip through the pages a bit. Some of you may even flip to the last chapter to see how the book ends. Of course, when you actually read the book, you still have reading work to do to make and extend meaning.

When friends recommend books, they often do more than summarize the plot, often telling you about the changes the characters undergo or the big ideas and themes, because these are the aspects that resonate with us. Then, when you read the book, you still have reading work to do to make and extend meaning.

Even in the case of rereading a book, you already know what it's about beforehand, but when you revisit it, you may focus on a different character, or read it from a more critical stance, inferring why the author made certain decisions. Your mind may be freed from constructing the plot or remembering how characters are related to notice new things, thinking about events and information in a new light, maybe even relating it to someone in your life. In other words, you still have reading work to do to make and extend meaning.

Regardless of how we've been introduced to texts, the meaning we enter with supports understanding and thinking rather than replaces it. When we introduce texts to young readers, our words, thoughts, and discussions guide them as they tap into their meaning-making process and support them in thinking about what the text might really be about.

*Organization helps a reader make meaning from what is written. When a reader is aware of the text structure being used, it helps him organize his thoughts as he proceeds through the text.*

—LAMINACK AND WADSWORTH (2015)

CHAPTER

4

# Considering How Books Work:
# TEXT STRUCTURES AND FEATURES

Think about your local grocery store—the one you've made so many trips to that you can zip in and out, gathering what you need with ease because you know and understand the organization so well. Frozen foods are on the right-hand side, so you begin on the left to prevent melting. You suddenly remember you need peanut butter and immediately head to the precise aisle where it's located without having to check the signs. You have smooth shopping experiences when you stop at stores in the same chain because they tend to be organized in a similar manner.

Then, one day, you visit a store from another chain. You walk through the door and pause. You glance around and quickly realize that this store doesn't work like the ones you're used to and you feel disoriented. But then you take a moment to survey the new situation and realize that you have the same goal—getting the items you need—so you change your navigational plan. It may take a little longer and you may have to backtrack if you passed something an aisle earlier. As you make your way through the store, however, you become more alert to signs and other signals that help you find the items you need.

Reading a text with a new structure may present similar challenges to our readers. When the text we plan to introduce works in ways students are familiar with, we don't need to include scaffolding with structure and features; students will be able to gather what they need with ease as they make sense from what they're reading. When a new book has a few confusing twists or interesting features, we can use the introduction to highlight signals that might guide the reader. After all, our goal is to help students understand the meaning of the entire book—the top line of the hierarchy of written language—so it makes sense that one of the first things we analyze is how the whole text is structured. We won't always need to show students how a book is organized, but sometimes not providing that support means students won't understand the story. The following example shows that understanding how a book works often makes or breaks a reader's ability to put ideas together.

As a second grader, Kath's son, Willie, was reading a book called *Weird Stories from the Lonesome Café* by Judy Cox (2001)—a chapter book at level M. He caught Kath's attention when he complained, "I don't get it. The boy and his uncle have a restaurant. There's Bigfoot and Elvis. I don't get it." Kath read a few chapters herself, skimmed the remainder, and reintroduced the book to him. She decided to lay out the structure for him so that he understood how the secondary characters fit into the bigger story.

"Each chapter introduces a new character," she said. "That character is a famous person from history, like Elvis, or a character from a movie or even a legend, like Bigfoot. All along, a group of reporters are trying to find an exciting story for their news show. You find out how the boy and his uncle help these mysterious characters, like Bigfoot, and how the mysterious characters help the boy and his uncle with their diner. It's like each chapter is its own little story, and there are also bigger stories, about the reporters or about making the diner successful, that connect all the chapters together."

Willie was a proficient reader, but understanding how the minor characters fit into the main idea was holding him back from accessing the story's central meaning. Knowing a bit about how those characters were introduced gave Willie a "map" for how the book worked, which enabled him to unlock the rest of the meaning on his own.

We don't have to be children's literature experts to properly introduce texts to students, but having an awareness of how texts are organized and function helps us anticipate supports students may need. As we plan, we ask, *How does this book work?* and *How does noticing how the book works help me navigate and understand what I'm reading?* We clue students in to how books are organized during the introduction so that they can do the work of incorporating ideas together. Eventually, this noticing will become automatic and students will begin to ask themselves questions about how books work, consider how structure affects the way they construct meaning, and adjust their reading accordingly.

This work brings us to the next phase in planning book introductions:

| |
|---|
| 1. Read the book for meaning. Think about what it's about and what it might really be about. Craft a meaning statement and a launching statement. |
| 2. Analyze how the book works (organizational structure and features). Plan how to support students (if necessary). |
| 3. Identify potentially challenging language structures and plan how to support students with them (if necessary). |
| 4. Determine words that may be difficult to solve (recognize or decode), or to understand (vocabulary), and plan how to support students with them (if necessary). |

Divided into two main sections, narrative and expository, this chapter explores a variety of ways that texts work with easier and more complex books. These examples are neither exhaustive nor meant to overwhelm, but rather are intended to open up your thinking and add to your repertoire of text analysis.

Figures 4.1 and 4.2 provide a menu of the various organizational structures and devices explained throughout this chapter. In each section, there are excerpts of book introductions to illustrate the thinking involved with connecting how a book works with meaning. Toward the end of the chapter, we briefly consider how book and print features affect the meaning of a text. We end with an example of a teacher thinking through planning and implementing a book introduction for a specific group of students.

Figure 4.1
NARRATIVE STRUCTURES
AND DEVICES

Figure 4.2
EXPOSITORY TEXT
STRUCTURES

| | |
|---|---|
| Plot<br>Backstory<br>Collection of short stories<br>Multiple events linked as one story<br>Simultaneous plotlines<br>Setting: passage of time<br>Setting: place<br>Narration and point of view | Single category-list<br>Categorical<br>Compare—contrast<br>Multiple text structures |

## HOW BOOKS WORK: STRUCTURES AND LITERARY DEVICES

In the literacy world, we use the same word, *structure*, to describe two levels of organization: how sentences are structured (often referred to as syntax, language structure, or grammatical structure) and how a book works (text structure). In Chapter 5, we will address *language structure* in further detail. Here, we turn our attention to how a book is organized by exploring various text structures in fiction and nonfiction, the relationship between the text and illustrations, book and print features, and the role these components play as they pertain to the work we do in book introductions.

Text structure refers to the ways authors present and organize information for the reader. It is a navigational tool that helps us work through a text, directing and sometimes rerouting us toward the construction of meaning. Cochran and Hain (2012) help us consider how important organization is to comprehending a text. "As readers interact with the text to construct meaning," they write, "their comprehension is facilitated when they organize their thinking in a manner similar to that used by the author. Readers who struggle with text comprehension often do so because they fail to recognize the organizational structure of what they are reading, and they are not aware of cues that alert them to particular text structures."

Structure can be influenced by genre, purpose, and crafting techniques. Overall, text structures typically fall into either narrative or expository categories. Within those broad categories, numerous substructures begin to emerge as text complexity increases. As we analyze the structure of books we plan to introduce, we ask ourselves, *How might aspects of this structure aid a reader's comprehension?* and *When following this structure, what might cause a reader to lose track of meaning?* Exploring these two questions gives us a sense of how to bring the components of text structure to the attention of readers during a book introduction so they might read with greater ease. Let's take a closer look at components of narrative and expository structures, starting with narrative.

## HOW NARRATIVE TEXTS WORK

In a traditional narrative, the story line, or plot, has the following structure: The main character has a problem or wants something, and tension rises as the character works to resolve that issue. A climax is reached and a turning point often occurs, which ultimately leads to a resolution and closure, whether the problem is neatly solved or not. Within that structure, we consider how the plot, setting (passage of time and place), narration, and point of view affect the meaning and organization of the story.

## Plot

To put the story together while reading, readers need to consider how the plot progresses. Lower-level texts usually follow a traditional linear plot progression with only one plotline. Beverley Randell, author of many guided reading texts, has written about the advantages that traditional story structure brings to the reader: "It gives motivation for reading and page turning. . . . Tension keeps interest alive. . . . It leads to satisfying endings. . . . It gives many opportunities for the development of logical thought, and the understanding of cause and effect" (2000, 9).

Students who have heard many stories with a conventional structure—problem, rising tension, climax, and resolution—may need little to no support during the introduction to discuss how the character might resolve the problem and follow the events as they read. As text organization becomes more complex, our questions shift to anticipate what might be tricky for readers. Are there parallel problems in the story? Are the events linked (as in Willie's book, *Weird Stories from the Lonesome Café*) or episodic (as in the Frog and Toad series)? The following range of plotline structures and devices are used by authors as texts become more complex.

### Backstory

Around level H, some texts provide a background of characters and events that precede the beginning of the primary story. It often sounds like an introduction, as in *Pterosaur's Long Flight*: "Long, long ago, two pterosaurs had a nest at the top of a big cliff. There were four baby pterosaurs in the nest. They had come out of their eggs a week ago" (Price 1997, 2). This narrative history continues for three more sentences before shifting to tell the book's main story about the search for food: "One warm morning, the father pterosaur took off from the top of the cliff to look for food" (4). The initial backstory often gives readers insight into how a character usually acts or what his or her life is normally like before shifting to focus on the story's main conflict. Noticing the transition from the backstory to *this* story alerts the reader that the familiar narrative text structure is about to begin.

### Collection of Short Stories

In Arnold Lobel's Frog and Toad books and Cynthia Rylant's Poppleton series, each chapter consists of its own short story that can stand alone. We can read one story, think about what it means, and move on to a different story about the same characters; we can even read the chapters out of order. In the end, we might draw some conclusions about the characters or notice that the stories all share a topic (e.g., seasons, friendship). This type of text structure doesn't usually need more than a quick mention to prepare readers (e.g., "Is this the type of book where it is one long story, like a movie? Or is it little episodes about the same group of characters, like a TV series?").

### Multiple Events or Chapters, Linked as One Story

In books such as those in Kate DiCamillo's Mercy Watson series or Kevin Henkes's Penny series, the chapters all tie together to tell a larger, more complex story with connected scenes that often reveals something bigger about the characters.

*Leroy Ninker Saddles Up* (DiCamillo 2014), a spin-off based on a character from the Mercy Watson series, works in a similar way. Leroy goes through trial after trial as he learns the responsibility of taking care of a beloved pet. Each chapter describes one event, but collectively they all work to tell a bigger story. Bringing this information to students' attention will help ensure that they think about how the events connect and develop into bigger ideas.

### Simultaneous Plotlines

Just as real life is layered with events, a character in a book might try to solve a bigger problem but encounter smaller issues to resolve along the way. Or, a character might want one thing throughout the whole book, and must deal with other situations to get to something bigger. In *Horrible Harry and the Triple Revenge* (2006) by Suzy Kline, Harry is mad at his friend Sid for ruining something that his other friend Song Lee made. Harry plots three different ways to get revenge against Sid for hurting Song Lee's feelings. The relationships among the various characters add layers to the plotline. The story isn't simply about Harry's revenge on Sid; it is also about the relationships between Song Lee and Sid, the class and Harry, Sid and Harry, and so on. The reader, along with the narrator, Doug, wonders if Harry is going too far with his defense of Song Lee. Will Sid realize that what he did was wrong? Will Harry ever forgive Sid? How might their relationships change? Pointing out multiple plotlines sets readers up to monitor each one as they read. It can also support building a theory about the characters and how they relate to each other.

Throughout this chapter, we provide several examples of how a teacher might analyze a text through the lens of text structure and plans to introduce it. These examples are excerpts, not full book introductions. Keep in mind that the text structure needs to be pointed out only if the teacher presumes it will enable the reader to better grasp the meaning.

Our first example explores supporting students with backstory, one of the plotline devices just described.

| **Example #1: Planning Book Introductions: Drawing Attention to Backstory** |
| --- |
| **Teacher's Thoughts About the Text** |
| *Henry and Mudge and the Sparkle Days* (Rylant 1988) is a level J text. The first chapter starts off with a general description of Henry and Mudge during the winter before telling the story about the first snowfall that year. The students about to read the book have heard *Henry and Mudge: The First Book* (1987) read aloud, so they are familiar with the characters. Each chapter of the new book describes a different event—playing in the snow, having a special dinner, going for a walk as a family. The connecting topics of the book are sparkling and winter—sparkling snow, lights in the house, lights in the sky. But a bigger idea is how much the family enjoys being together. |

---

**Excerpt of Introduction**

<u>Meaning statement and discussion about how the book works:</u> In some of Cynthia Rylant's books, she starts by giving an introduction, telling us how the characters usually act or what they like before she tells us a specific story. *Henry and Mudge and the Sparkle Days* (1988) is a collection of stories about how Henry's family enjoys winter together. Before Cynthia Rylant tells us those stories, she lets us know how the family usually behaves during winter. The author calls winter days "Sparkle Days." What do you think she means? (Discuss and look at pictures.) Listen to the first page of the first chapter, "Sparkle Days": "It was winter. Winter! Henry and his big dog Mudge loved winter, because Henry and his big dog Mudge loved snow" (5). (Discuss.)

The author tells us a little about Henry and Mudge in the wintertime. We keep reading and we find out how this winter, this specific story may be different from before. It says, "This winter they were still waiting for the first snow" (6). The words *This winter* are a clue that this little story is starting. Authors sometimes begin their chapters describing how things usually are, before starting to tell a little story, so that you can think about how the experiences in the story compare with what the characters are used to.

---

In this excerpt, the teacher begins with a link to the author's style. She shares what the author has done, why she likely did it, and how it helps the reader. Students can take what they learn about this generative understanding and apply it to other books they read that work in similar ways.

## Setting: Passage of Time

Writers often use time to organize and convey a message. We know from observing young children that as they grow, so too does their understanding of time and the vocabulary for describing it. For example, kindergartners may still mix up the words *yesterday* and *tomorrow* and need confirmation about weekends and school days. In *What a Writer Needs* (2013), Ralph Fletcher describes how young writers struggle to control time in their stories: "Most kids don't keep track of time. Unlike adults, children don't measure it, save it, parcel it out. . . . Children have trouble controlling time in their writing because they simply do not see it as an element to control. They are oblivious to it" (129). If Fletcher has noticed this in young writers, we imagine that young readers may be equally immature about perceiving time in the books they read.

Even with chronological time lines in narratives such as the one in *Father Bear Goes Fishing* (Randell 2006), readers need to fill in the gaps. Father Bear went off to catch fish. How much time passed by the time we read about Mother Bear and Baby Bear waiting for their supper? In this early-level text (D), there are no language connectors such as *A few hours later* to mark time—the reader needs to fill in that information. Some children may infer that without our help; others may need to be made aware of the passage of time to gain a fuller understanding of the bigger ideas in the story. As we support young readers with how books work, it's important to consider how the author and illustrator indicate time so that we can determine if it is explicit or if the readers need to infer it. Consider the following examples:

- *Indicated in illustrations*: Some illustrations show time of day, seasons, or other clues that time is passing. *You'll Soon Grow into Them, Titch* (Hutchins 1983) is about a brother who grows tired of receiving hand-me-downs. If you were to simply read the text, you might think the story took place over a day or two. But a close look at the illustrations reveals that months go by. Titch's mother becomes more and more pregnant, eventually bringing home a new baby. The birds out the window build a nest on one page and feed their babies on another. These subtle clues are key to understanding time, and the amount of time passing helps the reader understand that Titch's body is growing from the beginning to the end of the book.

- *Explicitly stated:* Authors often explicitly state how time passes in a story or tell what time it is by using transitional phrases. We start to see use of phrases that connect scenes around levels E and F: *The next day, A few hours later, One winter morning.* In some books, the story follows a pattern indicated by time. For example, *Carla's Ribbons* (Harper 1992) takes place over a week. Carla comes home from school every day missing a ribbon from her pigtails and can't figure out where they have gone. The author uses transitional phrases to connect the scenes: *On Monday, On Tuesday.* The passage of time contributes to the characters' increasing frustration with the mystery.

- *Identified through actions:* The narrative nonfiction text *Chameleon!* (2005) by Joy Cowley is about a chameleon in search of a meal: "Step by step, the chameleon creeps to the ground" (9), we read. We figure that time is passing slowly in this scene from the way the chameleon is moving. In *Henry and Mudge: The First Book* (1987) we infer that Henry searched for an extended period of time for his lost dog, Mudge: "So Henry walked and walked, and he called and called, and he looked and looked for his dog Mudge. He walked down one road, then down another road" (Rylant 1987, 30). In both examples, how the character moves through time matters to the heart of the piece. A chameleon is careful, searching for food and checking for danger. Henry was persistent in his search for his beloved Mudge.

- *Omission:* Writers leave stuff out. They have to. As teachers of writing, we work hard to shift students from writing every single thing that happens in a text to focusing on the important parts. As readers, we fill in the pertinent information that may need to be inferred. As reading teachers, sometimes it's necessary to guide students to ask, "How much time may have passed? What might have happened in between these two events?" Sometimes a reader needs to infer what happened, what was said, and what was thought between two scenes to understand a character's motivation or feelings.

The following excerpt from a book introduction demonstrates one way you might draw students' attention to the passage of time in illustrations while directly linking it to the meaning of the text.

---

**Example #2: Planning Book Introductions: Drawing Attention to Passage of Time**

**Teacher's Thoughts About the Text**

*You'll Soon Grow into Them, Titch* (1983) by Pat Hutchins is a level H story about the youngest child in a family who grows out of his current clothes but doesn't yet fit into his hand-me-downs. Multiple events follow a pattern as each sibling provides the boy with clothes they used to wear. Cueing in to the passage of time (and recognizing that Titch is on his way to being a big brother) will help readers understand the humor at the end of the book, when Titch finally gets a turn using a version of the line "You'll soon grow into them" with his newborn sibling.

In this example, the passage of time directly connects to the bigger meaning of the text and is worth attending to so students get the most out of it. The passage of time is subtle in this book and could be overlooked if the reader isn't tuned in to the clues in the illustrations.

---

**Excerpt of Introduction**

<u>Meaning statement:</u> Titch is the youngest kid in his family. Instead of getting something new when he grows out of his clothes, he gets hand-me-downs from his brother and sister. Take a look at why that's a problem. (*Hand out books. Discuss.*) Nothing fits him! Everyone tells him that he'll soon grow into the clothes, but as we know, that could take a long time.

---

<u>Discussion of how the book works</u>: Pat Hutchins uses the illustrations to give us clues about how much time passes during this story. Look at the birds out the window, the plants, or even Mom on a few different pages. What do you notice? (*Discuss. Birds build nests and baby birds hatch. Leaves grow and flowers bloom. Mom is pregnant, her belly gets bigger, and knits an outfit for a baby.*) So, you know this story is going to take place over at least a few months. Keep that in mind as you read and think about Titch's experiences.

---

Here, the teacher draws students' attention to a feature of how the book works (illustrations) but gives them the opportunity to notice what's significant about them. She then names for students what the illustrations mean for the passage of time and nudges them to keep that in mind as they read and think about what happens in the book.

The more you read with time in mind, the more you'll notice the subtle ways authors show how it passes. Ask yourself, *Is this something kids can figure out on their own, or do I need to draw attention to it in order to lead them to the bigger meaning of the text and begin to notice how other books work in similar ways?*

## Setting: Place

Where the story takes place is especially important when it affects the plot. In *Father Bear Goes Fishing* (Randell 2006), the setting is illustrated and described in text ("He went down to the river") on the first page. Mother Bear and Baby Bear are introduced for the first time on page 11 of the story through dialogue ("Where is Father Bear?"). The setting shows them standing at the foot of a curved path through a forest, with no river in sight. The reader uses the information that Baby Bear and Mother Bear are in a different location to infer that they are waiting for Father Bear to return home with their supper.

In early-level chapter books such as Cynthia Rylant's Henry and Mudge series and Kate DiCamillo's Mercy Watson books, illustrations clearly show where the scene is taking place and are often accompanied by a description of the setting in the text (e.g., from *Mercy Watson Goes for a Ride* [DiCamillo 2006, 2]: "Every Saturday after lunch, Mr. Watson goes outside. Mercy follows him. They stand in the driveway."). In chapter books with fewer illustrations, however, the reader sometimes needs to read a few paragraphs to figure out where a scene is taking place. Notice how the teacher points out where to gather information about how the setting changes in the excerpt from an introduction below.

---

**Example #3: Planning Book Introductions: Drawing Attention to Place**

**Teacher's Thoughts About the Text**

The first page of each chapter of the level M book *Ivy and Bean Break the Fossil Record* (Barrows 2007) doesn't explicitly let the reader know where the story is taking place. Sometimes the picture gives clues about where characters are, and other times dialogue or actions hint at where the story is taking place during a scene. For example, on page 2, the text refers to independent reading time: "She knew she wasn't supposed to talk during Drop Everything and Read." It isn't until page 9 that the setting is stated in the text: "All the other kids in Ms. Aruba-Tate's second-grade classroom were bent over their books."

By the time students reach level M, most have had experience inferring where each scene is taking place, but it depends on what their diet of books has been. Readers may need only a simple mention during the introduction to begin to ask, "Where are they now?" The reason setting matters in this story is that it correlates to the different behaviors and actions of the characters—they tend to act very differently at home versus at school, at recess versus during reading workshop.

**Excerpt of Introduction**

Meaning statement: Ivy and Bean's whole class is getting excited about a world record book that Bean is reading. Holding a record is when you're the best, first, or worst at something. The record could be anything from world's fastest woman to crazy ones like eating the most hot dogs. Ivy and Bean and their classmates are going to attempt to break some pretty interesting records. As you can imagine, some funny things happen when they try to become record-breakers. Anyone ever been interested in trying to break a record? (*Discuss*.)

Discussion of how the book works: We've been noticing that chapter books have only a few pictures per chapter. We get most of our information from the words now, with the pictures adding a little extra for us. One of the things I wondered when I read this book was where Ivy and Bean were in each chapter. Sometimes they were in the classroom, sometimes they were at recess, and sometimes they were at one of their houses. As I was reading, I kept asking myself, "Where are they now?" to help me understand why they were acting a certain way. We act differently in the classroom than we do at recess, right? Paying attention to where your characters are clues you in to why they might be behaving a certain way.

In this excerpt, the teacher began discussing how the book works by linking to what they already knew. She went on to share one of her wonderings and offered a specific strategy that helped her search for and monitor where the characters were and how the setting affected the events and actions of the characters. This was then generalized to a principle that readers could apply to numerous other books.

## Narration and Point of View

Recognizing who is telling the story helps the reader know whose perspective is driving it. If the text is written in first person, the narrated parts might give you a clue about that character's internal thinking. If it is written in second person, the writer draws us, the readers, into the piece. When a text is written in third person, the narrator often provides perspectives from multiple characters or includes descriptions of something that the characters might not know. Proficient readers quickly figure out who is telling the story. For readers who are expanding their repertoire of genres and text structures, the book introduction offers a place to let students know who is telling the story to support their understanding before they read.

A primary purpose of reading instruction is to help children internalize ways of thinking about texts. Eventually, we want students to approach texts asking, "Who is telling the story?" "Is it told from one point of view or multiple points of view?" "Is the narrator biased?" "How does knowing this help me make sense of what I'm reading?" to help them better understand and enjoy what they read.

In earlier-level texts, the pictures can play a huge role in determining point of view. Kath had been reading *The Walk* (Dufresne 2000) with students for years. However, it wasn't until Chrisie used the book in a professional development session to talk about the importance of illustrations in lower-level texts that she considered the narrator. Chrisie shared, "One page shows the dad's visual perspective—tops of the trees—and another shows the dog's view, picturing the leaves on the ground."

Suddenly Kath had an epiphany. "What?! *Gabby's* telling this story?"

Kath had ignored Gabby, the dog, as an essential character, and assumed that the narrator was a child (never pictured!). The recognition of who was telling this simple story changed how she introduced the book. It also added to her enjoyment of the book, knowing that the dog was, in essence, talking to the reader. More importantly, this experience teaches us to carefully read the pictures for perspective, time, and place, especially in the early levels.

| **Example #4: Planning Book Introductions: Supporting Narration and Point of View** |
| --- |
| **Teacher's Thoughts About the Text** |
| The level B book *The Walk* (Dufresne 2000) is part of a recurring Pioneer Valley series about a family and their dog, Gabby (not named in this book). Recognizing Gabby, we can name her in this early book, even though it is the first time students are meeting this character. Gabby is the narrator of the story and tells all the things she ("I") and Dad can see. Understanding who the narrator is ideally will support students with early monitoring by using meaning (from the pictures) and visual information (high-frequency words such as *Dad* and *I*). |
| **Excerpt of Introduction** |
| <u>Meaning statement</u>: Dad and his dog, Gabby, are out taking a walk. It's a beautiful day and they are noticing lots of things around them. Gabby is little and she is always noticing things low to the ground. But not Dad—he's looking up. He's tall! What kind of things can they see on their walk? (*Distribute books to students and discuss.*) |
| <u>Discussion of how the book works</u>: In this book, the dog is telling the story. Each picture helps us know what Gabby and Dad can see on the ground or higher up. Look at page 6. Who can see the rocks? That's right. Gabby said, "I can see the rocks." Say that with me. |

Here, the teacher tells how noticing point of view helps the reader, and then invites the readers to turn to a page and have a go using what she shared with them. This brief practice and rehearsal sets them up for success while reading that page, and sets them up to search pictures for meaning on other pages as they navigate the rest of the book.

Though we typically think of fiction texts when we consider narration and point of view, narrative nonfiction texts use these elements to provide perspective as well. *Chameleon!* (Cowley 2005), a narrative nonfiction text, describes the actions of the chameleon in such detail that the reader can imagine, just a bit, the challenges a chameleon faces when searching for a meal.

| |
|---|
| **Example #5: Planning Book Introductions: Drawing Attention to Point of View and Genre** |
| **Teacher's Thoughts About the Text** |
| *Chameleon!* (Cowley 2005), a level J text, is a nonfiction book written in narrative form. It tells the story of one chameleon in search of a meal. The chameleon wants something and has to overcome dangerous obstacles it encounters in the forest to get it. |
| **Excerpt of Introduction** |
| Meaning statement: In *Chameleon!*, the author, Joy Cowley, teaches us about chameleons—how they catch food, how they protect themselves from getting eaten, and how they attract a mate. |
| Discussion of how the book works: In order to teach us, Joy Cowley chose to tell us the story of one chameleon during one day of its life as it searches for food. (*Discuss.*) So this book works like a story—the chameleon is the character searching for food, and along the way he needs to make decisions about what is best to eat and how to protect himself. Take a look. |

Young readers often have more experience with expository nonfiction texts and might not yet realize they can learn from books that read like stories. They may expect information to be conveyed categorically or in other, more direct ways. This excerpt explains that while they will be reading a story, one of its main intentions is to inform them.

As students gain a firm grasp of narrative text structures and the elements that influence them, they apply their knowledge as they approach new and more advanced materials. In the same way, learning more about expository text structures helps students better navigate, learn from, and enjoy them. On to expository text!

(NOTE: To learn more about how books are organized, check out the chapter on series books in *Beyond Leveled Books: Supporting Early and Transitional Readers in Grades K–5*. It describes how thirty series are organized and includes possible teaching points to support in an introduction. The authors, Karen Szymusiak, Franki Sibberson, and Lisa Koch, describe the setup of each series and how they work [e.g., Elephant and Piggie, Mercy Watson, Stink, Cam Jansen].)

## HOW EXPOSITORY TEXTS WORK

In the earlier part of our careers, we taught guided reading with mostly narrative fiction texts. If students heard expository nonfiction, it was usually during a read-aloud with a text related to curriculum content or an interest of the class. Some of this was because we didn't know better at the time and some was because there weren't many expository texts written for guided reading groups. Now, publishers are pumping out leveled expository nonfiction texts and the quality is greatly improving. Lucky kids! These books explore topics children are typically interested in as well as introduce new topics to grow further areas of interest.

There is a difference in how one reads expository text versus narrative text. Expository texts are filled with facts and organized through structures such as categorical, chronological sequence, compare and contrast, or cause and effect. Each of these structures requires readers to slightly adjust their reading to gather and understand the information they're consuming. The challenge for the reader is in noticing variations in structures and knowing how to adjust their reading to accommodate for them. The challenge for teachers is to figure out ways to help students *use* these structures to elicit information. We don't point structures out just for the sake of pointing them out; we point them out so readers use them strategically as they read! If young readers aren't aware of these structures, then the very elements put in place to support them in making meaning might be something they are unable to access without help. The author thinks, "How can I organize this text so that the reader learns what I think is important, recognizes my message, and considers my viewpoint?" The reader subconsciously or consciously notices and uses the organizational structures to follow the author's line of thinking—learning, questioning, and connecting along the way. Our job, when introducing texts in small-group guided reading, is to notice the organizational structures and think, *Which structures might I need to point out to students, and how might I support them in using the structures so that they learn from this text more effectively?*

For example, Melissa Stewart's Which Animal Is Which? series guides readers to recognize the differences between animals that people often confuse (e.g., butterflies and moths, alligators and crocodiles) by comparing them. While introducing a book from this series, *Frog or Toad? How Do You Know?* (Stewart 2011), we might point out that it is organized in a way that compares a single aspect of the frog on the left side of the page with the same aspect of a toad on the opposite page to help us discriminate between the two animals.

In studying numerous guided reading texts, we have found that many early-level titles use only one structure (often categorical). This single-category structure focuses the text and enables the reader to more easily gather information around the focus of the content. So, a book may be all about different kinds of sharks, or all about the equipment you need to play tennis, or all about food groups that keep you healthy. At higher levels, and as the content typically becomes more complex, authors often use a combination of text structures to most effectively convey their points to the reader. For example, a book might have a few pages that show types of sharks (categorical) and another few pages that explain threats to their survival (cause and effect). Readers may need to navigate multiple structures and adjust their reading and thinking accordingly.

With this in mind, take a look at the analyses and excerpts of the following expository book introductions addressing a range of levels and structures. In each one, notice that the discussion of how a book works usually sets the reader up to explore big ideas. Also, note that this list doesn't include all categories (cause and effect, for example), but rather a sampling of the common structures we've encountered. Our hope is that highlighting a few texts will get you started thinking about how various expository texts are organized as you determine the degree to which the structure affects the students' ability to make meaning.

**Example #1: Planning Book Introductions: Drawing Attention to Single-Category Structure (List-Like)**

**Teacher's Thoughts About the Text**

The level C book *Baseball* (Finnigan 2006) uses a list-like structure to describe the type of equipment used in baseball. Barring the first and last sentences of the book, each sentence begins with the same sentence structure: "Here is _____ ." A big idea of the book is that there is specific equipment in baseball that you need to play the game.

**Excerpt of Introduction**

<u>Meaning statement:</u> Each sport has special uniforms and equipment that serve a purpose for the players. I know some of you play soccer and wear shin guards to protect your legs from getting kicked. What other equipment do you use? (*Discuss.*) The author of this book, *Baseball,* shows us all the things we need to play baseball.

<u>Discussion of how the book works:</u> It's almost as if the author is writing a list, one thing for each page: "Here is _____ ." "Here is _____ ." The last page is different—showing someone ready to play baseball!

In this example, the teacher names the overall structure that is used and alerts students to be aware of the slight variation in it on the last page.

**Example #2: Planning Book Introductions: Drawing Attention to Categorical Structure**

**Teacher's Thoughts About the Text**

*Fireflies* (Dufresne 2015b), a level E book, is a typical "all about" book centering on one topic. Unlike the baseball book, which is a list of things centered on the same topic (equipment), each page in *Fireflies* gives information in various categories about the insects.

| **Excerpt of Introduction** |
|---|
| <u>Meaning statement:</u> We start to see fireflies, or lightning bugs, at nighttime during July and August. A lot of kids try to catch them. (*Discuss.*) Before I read this book, I didn't know much more about them than how they twinkle in the summer. But this book taught me more about fireflies—it tells what they are, where they live, and what their life cycle is like. What are you wondering about fireflies that you hope you might learn from reading this book? (*Discuss.*) |
| <u>Discussion of how the book works:</u> Let me show you how this book works. Each section teaches us a different idea about fireflies. This first page tells about its name. On the next two pages we learn about the light they give off. Flip through and see what you might learn in other sections. |

By drawing students' attention to the categorical structure of the text, the teacher helps readers develop a framework for the information they'll read about. This framework not only helps them anticipate what they'll read, but it also assists in helping them summarize their reading and monitor when something doesn't fit with what they expect.

| **Example #3: Planning Book Introductions: Drawing Attention to Compare and Contrast** |
|---|
| **Teacher's Thoughts About the Text** |
| The level G book *Travel: Then and Now* (Yates 2008) uses a compare and contrast format, showing an example of a type of travel in the past and how that type of travel looks and works in the present. The illustrations are highly supportive (using black-and-white photographs from the past), and each sentence begins with either *Long ago* or *Today*. |
| **Excerpt of Introduction** |
| <u>Meaning statement:</u> We've been learning how things in the past—a hundred years ago, ten years ago, or one year ago—are different from the way they are today. People wore different clothes and they traveled differently. This book shows us how different travel was a long time ago compared with what we're used to these days. Take a look at some of these cool photographs. (*Discuss.*) |

Discussion of how the book works: Look at how this book works. On each of these two pages, the author compares how a type of transportation was in the past with how that same kind is today. One side shows an example of long ago. The other side shows nowadays, or today. Knowing this will help you think about how transportation has changed over time. Let's read and compare the ideas on these two pages.

Again, we see the teacher's identification of the text structure segue into how noticing it helps the reader think about and understand the text.

### Example #4: Planning Book Introductions: Drawing Attention to Multiple Text Structures

#### Teacher's Thoughts About the Text

Steve Jenkins and Robin Page's book, *What Do You Do with a Tail Like This?* (Jenkins and Page 2003), a level L book, begins with a brief introduction that speaks directly to the reader, explaining how the book works. Each section begins with close-up pictures of one specific body part (nose, ears, tails, eyes, feet, or mouth) of various animals and a question about how the animals use that part. The following two-page spread shows each animal in its entirety with an accompanying sentence that tells how that animal uses that body part. The last few pages of the book provide an overall description of each animal.

#### Excerpt of Introduction

Meaning statement: When you think about different kinds of animals you've seen, you know that many of them have similar body parts—nose, ears, tails, eyes—but have you ever stopped to think about how animals use these parts in different ways? (*Discuss.*) In this book, *What Do You Do with a Tail Like This?*, Steve Jenkins and Robin Page help us think about the unique and sometimes amazing ways animals use their bodies.

Discussion of how the book works: The authors did some cool things to interest us. They tell us how the book works on the first page. Let's read it together. (*Read.*) Now turn to the page with the close-ups of different tails. In each section, the authors ask us to guess how that body part is used. We also get to guess what animals those tails belong to. Can you guess? (*Discuss.*) Turn the page again. Now you can see the whole animals and read how each uses its tail. Turn to the last two pages. We see the same animals again, this time with more information about them overall.

After pointing out the author's introduction to *What Do You Do With a Tail Like This?*, the teacher took students to one section as an example of the way the text was set up. This provided an opportunity to discuss content, highlight print layout, and clear up any questions students may have had about how the book worked.

When we notice students struggling to read nonfiction texts, it is often because they do not know how to navigate the information. Selecting texts with different structures, providing instruction on how to navigate them, and discussing what students notice about structure and how it helps them understand, question, or monitor their reading aids them in learning more about how to use these navigational tools.

## BOOK AND PRINT FEATURES ACROSS GENRES

The structures and devices we've discussed so far are certainly the larger frameworks that determine how a book works, but other features also play a role in how we navigate, develop understandings from, and enjoy texts. Book and print features constitute the visual aspects of the text, including font, line breaks, page layout, illustrations, and other graphic features. They also include tools like the table of contents, index, diagrams, and charts. These features can affect how a reader accesses the message regardless of whether the text is narrative or expository, fiction or nonfiction. The idea isn't for students to just identify and name these features, but rather to learn how to *use them* to understand. We'll explore a few here.

### Font

A change in the type, color, or size of font often signals to readers that they need to pay close attention to something or read the text in a different way. For example, headings often stand out because they are bigger, boldfaced, or underlined. This cues the reader to start with the heading first and think about the content of that section. Words may be boldfaced, italicized, or enlarged to prompt the reader to read with more emphasis. Once introduced to these font features, many readers recognize them on their own and teachers can highlight them for a particular student or emphasize how to use them as a teaching point if meaning was impeded.

## Line Breaks

Have you noticed a progression in how sentences are laid out across the page as you move up the levels? Many publishers support students with phrased reading by breaking lines at the end of meaningful phrases through level E. The white space at the end of one line, followed by a return to the left side of the next line, helps facilitate natural pausing and phrasing. This visual support starts to drop off as readers begin to match phrasing based on meaning and punctuation rather than heavily relying on the white space provided by line breaks. Students may benefit from practicing how to use line breaks to help them group words in meaningful units.

## Page Layout

With this characteristic, we ask, "How easily can children locate and follow the text on the pages?" In early-level books, the text and illustrations are consistently placed on the pages—typically with the words on the first page of a two-page spread and a photograph or illustration on the other, or with the photograph or illustration at the top of the page and the text at the bottom. Many readers of early-level texts rely as much on the illustrations as the text, as illustrations are easily accessible and carry much of the meaning. When young readers are learning to attend to print, it's helpful for them to be able to anticipate that the text will be in the same place every time the page is turned. However, as text complexity increases, so do the variations of where the text and graphics are located. We consider this placement, why text and visual aids are placed where they are, and whether or not students need help noticing how to follow the flow before planning our introductions.

## Illustrations

The power of illustrations is discussed earlier in this chapter as well as in Chapter 3. Illustrations give clues about time and perspective, and can show things close-up or as part of a bigger scene. Sometimes illustrations confirm what is stated in the text and sometimes they add additional information. As we prepare our introductions, we determine whether readers need support attending to or inferring from illustrations to enhance their understanding of the plot and main ideas.

## Graphic Features

Diagrams, charts, graphs, time lines, maps, and other graphic aids can be used to show details, understand the order of events, compare information, illustrate where something occurred, and more. Authors use these features to highlight pertinent information. During book introductions, we direct students' attention to or scaffold interpretation of these features so readers might consider how the information they convey fits with or enhances understanding of the overall content.

# PULLING IT ALL TOGETHER

We've included several partial excerpts from book introduction plans to illustrate how specific text structures and characteristics might be introduced. Now, to get a more integrated view, we'll listen in as our colleague Jen Baskette-Tierney introduces an expository text to a group of students in June of their kindergarten year. You may want to reference her planning sheet (Figure 4.3) and compare it to how the lesson played out in real time.

---

**Teacher's Thoughts About the Text and Students**

*All About Ants* (Dufresne 2013) is a level J nonfiction book that may convey the bigger idea that although we often consider ants to be pests, they are complex and interesting creatures. The text is organized by categorical sections and includes a table of contents. Each section describes a different aspect of ants (e.g., types of, communication, life cycle). A few diagrams are used throughout the book to illustrate and expand on the parts of the ant and the ant life cycle.

The students in this group are confident readers who have some experience with reading nonfiction books. Despite their experience, this book was one of the first they would read with a table of contents in guided reading. When reading previous nonfiction books, two members of the group sometimes looked at diagrams but didn't always read the labels, neglecting to gather the pertinent information they provide. With this in mind, some guidance with how the book is organized and the role that diagrams play in the book may be needed.

Figure 4.3

JEN BASKETTE-TIERNEY'S PLANNING SHEET FOR *ALL ABOUT ANTS*

**Group/Students:**   Raheem, Elias, Annie     **Date:**     June 5

**Running Record Student:**   N/A     **Running Record Book/Level:**     N/A

**New Book/Level:**   All About Ants, Level J

**Introducing the Text:**

*Meaning Statement:*

It's almost summertime, time for ants to come out. I usually think of ants as pests and try to get rid of them, but this book, <u>All About Ants</u>, has me thinking in a new way.

*Support (how book works, language structure, words):*

Table of contents, p. 14, diagram—show how words and pictures work together to inform

p. 4, diagram—students discuss

*Launch:*

See what the information in this book leaves you thinking about ants.

**Anecdotal Notes:**

| Student: Raheem | Student: Elias | Student: Annie |
|---|---|---|
| | | |
| Student: | Student: | Student: |
| | | |

**Text Discussion:**
So what are you thinking about ants now? What made you think that/change your opinion?

**Group Teaching Point:**
Compare what they knew about ants with what they now know. Support thinking with evidence from the text.

**Word Work:**
Changing the y to i and adding -es to make some words plural

| MS. BASKETTE-TIERNEY | So, we've been reading nonfiction books to learn about different animals. We've read about alligators and crocodiles and porpoises and dolphins and compared them with each other. I've got a new book to share with you that will teach us about ants. It's almost summer and things are getting warmer outside, and you know who comes out when the weather gets warm— |
|---|---|
| RAHEE | Ants! |
| ELIAS | Ants! |
| ANNIE | And bugs! |
| MS. BASKETTE-TIERNEY | You've probably seen ants at your house or in other places. |
| ANNIE | Yesterday— |
| ELIAS | Tons. They follow a line, inside this hole, into this little hole in my house. |
| ANNIE | Yesterday, I saw like one million ants. |
| ELIAS | I tried to wash them away with water. |
| MS. BASKETTE-TIERNEY | We always try to get rid of these ants, don't we? At least I do in my house, but you know what this book helps us think about? That ants are pretty amazing little insects. |
| ANNIE: | They are nature. Insects are nature. |
| MS. BASKETTE-TIERNEY | They are part of nature. And— |
| RAHEEM | I saw one on my table at school. |
| MS. BASKETTE-TIERNEY | —and there are over 12,000 different types of ants and they live all over the world. |
| ANNIE | I think I know one—the honeypot ant? |
| RAHEEM | Or a red ant. Or just a regular ant? |
| MS. BASKETTE-TIERNEY | Well, we're going to see about some different ants in this book. This book is called *All About Ants* and it has something special that lets us know how it's organized. Let's open up to the first page. This is called the table of contents, and it tells you everything you can read about in this book.<br><br>There's a section called "Ants Are Everywhere." They have ant colonies; that's where they live. Take a look at the table of contents and see what else you might read about. |

| RAHEEM | Communication. (*Reads.*) "Ant Communication." |
|---|---|
| ELIAS | There is a glossary. |
| ANNIE | The index is on 20. |
| RAHEEM | "Helpers or Pests?" I think it's a helper. |
| ELIAS | What's this? "The Life Cycle of an Ant." |
| MS. BASKETTE-TIERNEY | When you read each part in the table of contents, you can start to think about what you'll learn in each section. So we're going to read about lots of different kinds of things. Which ones are you most interested in? |
| RAHEEM | Um, colonies? |
| ELIAS | It goes like this, 2, 4, 6, but there's no 8. It goes 2, 4, 6, 10, 14, 16, 18, 20. |
| MS. BASKETTE-TIERNEY | So you're noticing—these are the pages you can turn to and start finding that information. What are you excited to turn to? Which part are you interested in? |
| ANNIE | "Ant Communication," because I have no idea about that. |
| MS. BASKETTE-TIERNEY | How about you? (*Nods to Raheem, who points to a heading.*) "The Life Cycle of an Ant?" Let's turn to that. What page does "The Life Cycle of an Ant" start on? |
| RAHEEM | Page 14. |
| MS. BASKETTE-TIERNEY | Let's all turn to page 14. Another feature this book has is diagrams, which teach us more about the subject. |
| STUDENTS | (*Point to and talk about parts of the graphic.*) |
| MS. BASKETTE-TIERNEY | Notice it has the name of this section written up the side, "The Life Cycle of an Ant," and then it has some words (*reads first sentence*). And then it has this thing called a diagram, which puts words and pictures together to show us more. See how they put these pictures in a circle? This type of diagram (*points*) shows us the cycle an ant goes through as it grows up. So if you look here, what's that a picture of? |
| ALL | An ant. |
| MS. BASKETTE-TIERNEY | It says, "Adult: The pupa emerges as an ant." And you know what ants, do? They lay— |
| ALL | Eggs! |

| MS. BASKETTE-TIERNEY | It says, "Egg: Ant eggs are oval in shape." And then it goes to larva, then it goes to pupa, and then it goes to (*points*)— |
|---|---|
| ANNIE | Adult— |
| MS. BASKETTE-TIERNEY | An adult ant. So this is called a diagram and this one helps us picture how an ant grows from an egg to an adult. Turn to page 4. |
| RAHEEM | All right. I'm on page 4. |
| MS. BASKETTE-TIERNEY | So here's another diagram. What do you think this one will show you? You can turn and talk. |
| RAHEEM | The parts of an ant. |
| ELIAS | (*To Annie*) This is what it looks like. |
| ANNIE | That's the abdomen? |
| RAHEEM: AND ANNIE | (*Singing to the tune of "Head, Shoulders, Knees, and Toes"*) Head, thorax, abdomen, abdomen! |
| MS. BASKETTE-TIERNEY | Is it the abdomen? Let's look at the diagram. How is it written for this picture (*points*)? |
| ALL | (*Reading*) Abdomen, thorax, head. |
| MS. BASKETTE-TIERNEY | The author shares some really interesting information about ants with us. I can't wait to hear what you're thinking about ants after you read this book. |

Jen Baskette-Tierney's explanation of the table of contents and diagrams supported students' navigation of the text, which likely contributed to their growing understanding of how complex those pesky little ants crawling around our kitchens are. Their previous understanding of the content, combined with new information they learned from the book, led to interesting discussion after they read. The kids asked questions of each other, used the table of contents to quickly refer to interesting details (ants have two stomachs!), and asked deeper questions about the life cycle of an ant ("What happens when the queen dies?"). Jen set her readers up to *use* how the book works to learn about ants, which in turn set the stage for how they may approach other nonfiction books with similar organization and features in the future.

This chapter adds another layer to our planning process: after determining meaning, we examine how a book works as a whole to help access that central meaning. The following chapters add two more layers to the planning process.

You may wonder just how much to include in a book introduction. The answer really lies in how you answer this question: *How might I support this group of students—briefly—so that they can access the meaning when they read the text?* There are no hard and fast rules. Our ultimate goal is to help readers construct meaning at the highest level of the hierarchy of written language. If we feel confident that students are familiar with the way the new text works, we simply move on; there's certainly no need to include every component in the introduction. Yet when we notice that the book may be like our visits to a grocery store from a new chain, with different organization or new features, we help readers navigate the text as needed with the intent of supporting them with the knowledge and strategic actions necessary to develop big ideas and wonderings about it.

*Hearing new language structures, and perhaps
especially repeating them—always in the context of
the book and its illustrations as a whole—make it
that much more likely that they will be assimilated
into the child's expansion of his invisible, internal,
English language system.*

—COURTNEY CAZDEN (2004)

# CHAPTER
# 5

# Considering Language Structure:
# ORAL LANGUAGE, SYNTAX, AND SENTENCE COMPLEXITY

Like us, you probably recognize story language in books that might challenge readers. You flag phrases such as *"Once upon a time"* or "Off they went!" and give kids an opportunity to hear and say them a few times, running them "through the ear and across their tongues" before reading them independently (Clay 1998, 174).

Storybook phrases aren't the only structures that trip up readers. A few years ago, our district's Reading Recovery teacher leaders helped expand our notion of how language structures support and challenge students. Through their guidance, we started to notice the subtle syntactical challenges for very beginning readers, English learners and native English speakers alike, by studying students' responses, errors (miscues), and hesitations. We looked at reading errors and noticed that, often, it may have been the context—the sentence or the phrase housing the word—that caused the confusion. These experiences broadened our definition of what might be structurally challenging for students. For example, moving from a level B text ("I like to read to my mom. I like to read to my dad") to a level C text ("'Come with me,' said Mom"), readers may encounter dialogue for the first time, perhaps making an error such as "Come with me, *Sam* Mom" (substituting *Sam* for *said*). Some of those students may have heard a volume of books with dialogue; others may have only begun to develop a listening language for stories with dialogue in English. Regardless of these previous experiences, many students may need support the first few times they read dialogue themselves.

As awareness of such challenges evolved, we expanded our notion of what constitutes complexity in language structures. In higher-level-texts, for example, readers encounter new language structures through sentence complexity—longer sentences that include introductory or embedded clauses, compound sentences, or multiple adjectives. Something as simple as the comma can be challenging because of its many uses. Book introductions can include opportunities for students to "rehearse" a sentence once or twice to mimic the cadence or phrasing of meaningful chunks. This allows the reader to hold on to multiple ideas or experience processing a more complex sentence such as this one from a level I text: "One very hot morning, Nelson's wise old grandmother took all the elephants past the water hole and down to a mud pool" (Randell 1997, 4).

In Chapter 4, we studied how books work, examining various text structures that authors use. In this chapter, we narrow our idea of structure a bit more by considering it through the lens of how words are put together in phrases and sentences and the effect this may have on students' ability to make sense of the text.

Readers use knowledge of how English works and what they've heard spoken and read to search for information in their reading and monitor whether their reading sounds right. All readers are language learners to some degree. Even adults stumble when they encounter something their ear hasn't been attuned to yet. To empower readers to access the meaning of unfamiliar language structures and complex sentences, we analyze texts with the students' oral language abilities in mind so that we may anticipate what might be new or unusual for them. Then, we can consider how to support readers with those language structures that fall outside of their oral language use. This chapter will help you do just that as we explore

- what syntax is and how readers use it,

- a process for analyzing language structure complexity when planning a book introduction, and

- suggestions for supporting readers in noticing and using language structure.

Even though this chapter is specifically about language structure, notice—as always—how meaning connects to each section and remains at the forefront of our interactions with children.

# SYNTAX: HOW LANGUAGE WORKS AND SOUNDS

We use the term *language structure* to refer to grammar, sentence structure, or syntax: the way words are put together in rule-governed ways. The concept of syntax, or language structure, connects directly to the work many of us do when analyzing running records. To make sense of texts, readers use any combination of three main sources of information while reading: meaning, structure, and visual. Errors and self-corrections during a running record are coded M, S, or V to give us a clear view of the sources of information used or neglected to make attempts and problem-solve while reading:

- M—meaning or semantics. The reader uses pictures, context, and background knowledge to consider a sensible possibility.

- S—structure. The reader uses syntax or what sounds grammatically correct in the English language.

- V—visual or graphophonemic information. The reader uses the print on the page: the letters and the sounds they make, parts of words, and whole-word units.

Regardless of your level of expertise in analyzing running records, you already know that children unconsciously use their strong sense of language structure to know what sounds syntactically correct. A reader may substitute a past-tense verb for another past-tense verb ("She *rushed* to the car" instead of "She *ran* to the car") or a noun for a noun ("Mom gave him a *truck*" instead of "Mom gave him a *toy*"). Or they may substitute different parts of speech that also sound right ("The dog was *running* fast" instead of "The dog was *really* fast"). Readers use their sense of language structure in strategic ways.

## Searching for and Using Language Structure

Readers may search for and use language structure to anticipate what might sound right in their reading (often indicated by pausing or rereading). This helps them make a syntactically appropriate attempt by pulling from their developmental oral language structure. As Marie Clay puts it, "We do this kind of predicting as listeners when we follow the speaker and often almost finish his sentence for him. The child has the same kind of control over syntactic prediction at the level of his own language usage" (Clay 1991, 293). Readers become more adept at this searching and predicting behavior the more they are exposed to and use a variety of language structures. This, of course, occurs when they have numerous opportunities to engage in conversations and read a variety of books. In doing so, their knowledge of the English syntactic system deepens and their repertoire of language possibilities to consider and search for while reading broadens.

## Monitoring and Correcting with Language Structure

Readers listen to themselves. They check what they've read with what they've heard, spoken, or read in the past. They ask themselves, *Does it sound right? Can we say it that way in English?* For example, a reader may mistakenly read, "It was *rain* outside," prompting his awareness of language structure to send up a red flag. He then hesitates or stops because his reading doesn't sound right. As a result of this monitoring, we would hope that he would then search for more information, perhaps rereading to think about what word might sound better in the sentence (structure), looking closely at the last part of the word (visual), and checking the picture to confirm that it still makes sense (meaning), to then self-correct: "It was *raining* outside."

## Reading Fluently

Fountas and Pinnell describe six dimensions of fluency: pausing, phrasing, stress, intonation, rate, and integration. Awareness and use of language structure factor into each of these dimensions, especially when it comes to pausing and phrasing. "Pausing refers to the way the reader's voice is guided by punctuation. . . . Phrasing refers to the way readers put words together in groups that represent meaningful units of language" (2006, 69). Proficient readers group words into phrases that sound right and make sense, and attend to punctuation that assists with this.

Let's return to the example from the beginning of this chapter: "One very hot morning, Nelson's wise old grandmother took all the elephants past the water hole and down to a mud pool" (Randell 1997, 4). The comma assists the reader with the first phrase, but after that, the reader needs to rely on meaning to group words into meaningful phrases: descriptions of the grandmother, the first place she took them, and the second place she took them. An awareness of language structure helps readers group the words into meaningful phrases, which supports integration of all dimensions of fluency.

## Inferring the Meaning of Concepts or Vocabulary

Readers use language structure along with meaning to gain an idea about what a new word or phrase means. For example, a reader may be familiar with the word *please* as an adverb, but may become confused when encountering it in a new context: "I am *pleased* that you were able to come." The reader thinks, "What might that word mean when used in this way?" Then the reader may mentally replace it with a familiar word that makes sense and sounds right in context: "I am *glad* that you were able to come." All of this happens very quickly and results in the reader learning the meaning of the word (*pleased*) in the new context.

# A PROCESS FOR IDENTIFYING POTENTIALLY CHALLENGING STRUCTURES

To review, we plan introductions by reading texts through multiple lenses: the meaning lens, the text structure lens, the language structure lens, and the lens of the child's or group's oral language and reading abilities. Anticipating challenging phrases or sentence structures is the next step in the process of crafting meaningful book introductions:

| |
|---|
| 1. Read the book for meaning. Think about what it's about and what it might really be about. Craft a meaning statement and a launching statement. |
| 2. Analyze how the book works (organizational structure and features). Plan how to support students (if necessary). |
| 3. Identify potentially challenging language structures and plan how to support students with them (if necessary). |
| 4. Determine words that may be difficult to solve (recognize or decode), or to understand (vocabulary), and plan how to support students with them (if necessary). |

When it comes to syntax, there are layers of what might be challenging or supportive to the reader. These layers depend on the readers' oral language development as much as on how simple or sophisticated the text is. This means we need to know our students as language users, analyze the language structures in books we plan to introduce, and compare the two in relation to one another to determine potential structural challenges for readers. Then, even after our preparation, we must recognize that we still might have to support students throughout the lesson as needs arise.

## Considering Readers' Use of Language Structures

As always, we begin thinking about what may be challenging by starting with what we know about our students. We use what we know about the way our students talk and how they've processed language structures in previously read texts to carefully consider language structures they are aware of and can use with ease.

Formal descriptions and assessments of language proficiency such as WIDA Performance Definitions, as described in *2012 Amplification of the English Language Development Standards* (2014, 8–9) and Marie Clay's *Record of Oral Language* (2015) can be used when necessary to think about and assess students' oral language use. Guides such as these might be helpful and informative, but a more common and practical method for analyzing speech patterns is kid-watching. Pay attention to a child's speech patterns during informal and formal situations. Listen in during a "turn and talk" or during a buddy reading. Attend to how the child responds when you engage in reading and writing conferences. When a child tells you about his or her weekend on Monday mornings, take note of the longest sentence he or she says. This awareness will help you judge which language structures a child may use to support reading (e.g., to help predict the next word in a phrase) and which he or she may need support with.

### Consider Students' Expanding Language Systems

Speakers of all languages, whether native or not, continue to expand their grammatical structures throughout their lives. As we become more sophisticated speakers, listeners, readers, and writers of a language, we adjust to what sounds right. Knowing what stage our learners' language systems are in can help us anticipate any challenges that might come up when they're reading.

When Kath's daughter, Charlotte, was five and a half, this is how she orally explained an experience in a bounce house: "I was felling down and hurted myself on the scratchy part." She knew that the past tense of *fall* is *fell*, but didn't realize that the gerund is *falling* in present or past tense. She generalized adding *-ed* to make a verb past tense and didn't realize that the past tense of *hurt* is still *hurt*. When reading, she did not notice the dissonance when she read "Yesterday, two children *come* to play." Yet when offered both choices—"Which sounds right: 'Two children *came* to play' or 'Two children come to play?'"—she recognized that "Two children *came* to play" sounded right. In other words, she may not have been able to generate the correct use of many past-tense verbs on her own, but she was beginning to recognize what sounded more correct.

An expanding sense of language structure can also present itself when a bilingual student is using patterns held over from her primary language rules. Consider the following exchange between two adults (one a native English speaker, the other not).

> **PERSON 1:** So after waiting an hour, he finally got there. I really wanted to talk with him, but it was late and I was exhausted!
>
> **PERSON 2:** What time did he *came*?—I mean, *come*?

Person 2 quickly self-corrected her use of *came.* In English, when asking a question about something in the past, you use the present form of the verb: "Where did you *go* last night?" In Spanish, by contrast, the past tense is used, which makes a whole lot of sense because it is consistent with asking about something that happened in the past: "¿Donde *fuiste*?" Unlike Charlotte, the speaker in this example was able to monitor and quickly correct herself.

As you can see, teachers have multiple opportunities to informally assess their students' general language use. The next step is to keep students' common language development in mind while analyzing texts to determine which structures and sentences might support the reader and which might be challenging.

## Analyzing Sentence Complexity and Language Structures in Text

Have you ever heard a child use a phrase for the first time and thought, "Whoa, when did he learn that phrase? Do I say that?" Children learn from each other, from songs, movies, and books, and from interactions with parents and teachers. Their capacity to learn language is vast. In preparing to introduce a text in a small group, we need to be open to which language structures might be new to them so we can help them take the structures on. Our job is to support students not only in saying new structures, but also in understanding what they mean and how they connect to the larger units of the book. The following are a few possibilities to consider.

## New Language Structures and Sentence Complexity

As you peruse books looking for ones to match with your readers, notice the complexity of sentences. Keep in mind the language structures your students already know, what you may need to support during the introduction, and what you might leave for reading work. Employing these three categories keeps us in check when leaving work for students to do by reminding us that we also have opportunities to support by teaching or prompting while students are reading if necessary. However, if we find that a book may pose numerous linguistic challenges for a group of readers, it could be that it's too difficult for them at this point in time.

## Vernacular

Language in books may not reflect the way a particular group or region communicates. For example, there is a series of books developed in New Zealand where a babysitter "looks after" children. Readers may be unfamiliar with that phrase, because in their culture, babysitters are referred to as *taking care of* children. Even a reader who can read and write the word *after* may stumble over such a phrase at first because it is used in a different way. Proficient readers can read new phrases and infer new meanings. Those who are less proficient, however, sometimes doubt that they've solved, or decoded, a word correctly because it doesn't sound right to them (yet) and they need some support with confirming their attempt (e.g., "You read it right. It means took *care of.*").

## Literary Language

Most of us are aware of the difference between literary language and our everyday speaking language. Thus, we are supportive of children as they encounter story language such as "Down the dusty road and far away, a poor mother once lived" (Wood and Wood 1987) in their instructional texts. The trick is determining the subtleties of what might be literary language at the lower levels. To many readers, phrases like *after all* and *she cried and cried* don't seem like literary language because we have already adopted them into our speech. Younger readers may need help realizing that the latter phrase means "she cried for a long time." Although our goal isn't to cover every single phrase that might be new to students, our awareness of what might be novel readies us to dip in and support readers before, during, or after their reading.

### *Familiar Words in Unfamiliar Language Structures*

A colleague once said to Kath, "I don't understand. This child read the word correctly on this page, but missed it two pages later. He knows the word *up*!" The student could write the word *up* and had read it correctly in multiple books. However, in this book he stopped and appealed to the teacher at the word when he read the sentence, "The boy walked up to the tree." On the surface, it appeared that the student did not know how to read this common high-frequency word. But a closer look at the text revealed that *up* was used in a language structure that was unfamiliar to the student. The word *up* in the phrase *walk up to* means "to approach on foot." There were a few possibilities for why the child stopped based on how the word was used in the sentence. He might have been thinking of the most common meaning of up. In that case it would have sounded better to read, "The boy walked up the tree" (meaning "The boy climbed the tree"). Or he may have predicted that the sentence would say, "The boy walked to the tree" but then stopped because he noticed the word *to* was not directly after the word *walked*. Either way, the teacher assumed that the child appealed for help because he didn't know how to read the word *up*. Yet it's possible that there was a mismatch between what he saw on the page and what he thought should've been on the page.

In *Becoming One Community* (2004), Kath and Suzanne provide a chart with examples of potential structural challenges for readers (84–85). Figure 5.1 includes more examples to foster thinking about unfamiliar language structures.

Figure 5.1
POTENTIAL STRUCTURAL CHALLENGES

| Type of Sentence Complexity or Language Structure | Examples from Text | Meaning |
|---|---|---|
| Story language or literary language | *Once upon a time* | It happened in the past; it isn't clear exactly how long ago. |
| | *"His back went up!"* (Smith 2001) | The author is describing how a cat's back arches when it is mad or scared. |
| | *on and on* | Continuing |
| | *at last, after all* | Finally |
| Sentence complexity<br><br>-length of sentence<br><br>-description<br><br>-verb tense<br><br>-dialogue | *"Baby Bear ran to get the big white mushroom."* (Randell 1994) | The writer is describing the mushroom with two adjectives. |
| | *"Her toe poked out of one, the laces were almost black, and the tongues hung sideways, worse than a slobbery dog."* (McDonald 2013) | The writer is describing her shoes, using a list in the form of a sentence. |
| | *"You woke me up!"* | *Woke* is an irregular conjugation of *to wake*. Kids might want to say *waked*. |
| | *"Look at me," said Susie. "I made a very tall tower."* | Susie said both sentences. |

*(continues)*

*(continued)*

| | | |
|---|---|---|
| Reference of preposition | *He walked up to the tree.* | *Walked up* to signifies approaching. |
| | *He went up the tree.* | *Went up* signifies climbing. |
| Reference of pronoun or noun | *I could not see her because it was in the way.* | Describe what the word *it* refers to (whatever is blocking the view of the narrator). |

## Level of Sophistication

The chart in Figure 5.1 is only a sampling of sentence complexity factors that may be structurally challenging for readers. You'll also want to consider the various levels of sophistication in many of the categories. To illustrate, consider this continuum of how dialogue becomes more complex:

- Speaker tag after the dialogue: *"Look at me!" said Mom.*

- Speaker tag before the dialogue: *Mom said, "Look at me!"*

- Use of alternative verb in the speaker tag: *"What a mess!" she complained.*

- Varied placement of the verb: *"Where are you?" Mom shouted. "Where are you?" shouted Mom.*

- Use of pronoun: *"Where are you?" she shouted.*

- Speaker tag breaking up two different sentences: *"Look at me," said Susie. "I made a very tall tower."*

- Action or description added to speaker tag: *"Where do you think you're going?" she asked as she leaned in and scowled.*

- Speaker tag breaking up one sentence: *"Do you think," she asked, "that they realize where he is hiding?"*

- Line space or indented paragraphs between what two characters say:

> *"Where is Baby Bear?"*
> *said Mother Bear.*
> *"Father Bear,*
> *is Baby Bear with you?"*
>
> *"No," said Father Bear.*
> *"Where is he?"* (Randell 1996, 9)

- Use of pronouns in a longer conversation or lack of speaker tags; the reader needs to keep track of who is saying what:

> *"I don't know," Astrid said. "She didn't tell me."*
> *"Well, that's not a good sign," I said, "Yet*
> *another secret."*
> *"Another secret?" she asked.*
> *"Yes," I said.*
> *"What other secrets were there?" she asked.*
> *"Remember what she bought at the bazaar?"*
> *I asked.*
> *"Oh yeah," Astrid whispered. "I forgot that started*
> *out as a secret."*

As you can see, we can't assume that because readers have experience with reading dialogue, they won't ever need support with dialogue again. By noticing the growing levels of sophistication in dialogue and other areas of language structure, we heighten our awareness of what might be unusual to students, which then helps us anticipate where to offer support.

## PULLING IT ALL TOGETHER

After considering the developmental language of our readers and the language structures in books, the next step is to compare the two to determine which structures may be potentially challenging to read. To illustrate this process, we'll use an example of how Kath planned an introduction for a group of first graders. First, we describe the developmental language of the group and the language structures in the selected text, *Blackberries* (Randell 1996). Then, you'll see how Kath thinks through which language structures to address in the book introduction.

| Planning a Book Introduction: Drawing Attention to Language Structure |
|---|
| **Teacher's Thoughts About the Text and Students** |

The four students in this group are just moving from level D to level E texts. All four are fluent English speakers. Michelle speaks both English and Spanish, though English seems to be her dominant language. Caroline is young and still makes errors such as "He *throwed* the ball." Though she may not be able to generate the correct use of many past-tense verbs yet, she is beginning to recognize which sounds right if you offer her two choices. Peter reads word by word, only beginning to put two and three words together (e.g., "said Mom"). Caroline and Michelle read in two- and three-word phrases. Peter and Daniel seem to have well-developed language structure for their ages, so Kath doesn't anticipate issues with language structures in the new text. Daniel is the strongest reader of the group. He may be moved to another group soon.

Kath chose to introduce *Blackberries* (level E) because the students had previously read and enjoyed another book with the same characters. In this book, Mother Bear and Father Bear are worried that they have lost Baby Bear but he is nearby, stuffing himself with blackberries. Possible big ideas are little children sometimes get distracted and don't pay attention to the rules or safety (this is probably more relevant to kids) and parents need to always keep track of their younger children (this is probably an adult perspective). Because this text follows a typical narrative structure, there are no anticipated issues to consider regarding how the book works.

There are several language structures in this book that grab Kath's attention. The first page of *Blackberries* has one sentence printed over four lines of text. The next page shows a picture of three baskets (large, medium, and small). The sentence next to each basket describes which basket each bear will put its blackberries into. Kath doesn't think these students will have a hard time with these pages as long as they understand that the bears are preparing to go blackberry picking. If less proficient English learners were in the group, it may be worth pointing out the apostrophe s ('s) and rehearsing one of the phrases (e.g., "Mother Bear's blackberries") or listening in as the child reads that page and providing support if needed.

The next few pages are as follows:

| Page 7 | Excerpt from the Text | What Kath Noticed and Considered |
|---|---|---|
| | "Blackberries, blackberries, I like blackberries," said Baby Bear. | Baby Bear talks to himself in a singsong nature. The picture shows that the other characters aren't looking at him or near him. He is sitting down among the blackberry bushes. |

| Page 9 | "Where is Baby Bear?" said Mother Bear.<br><br>"Father Bear, is Baby Bear with you?"<br><br>"No," said Father Bear. " Where is he?" | The comma after the phrase *Father Bear* alerts the reader that Mother Bear is addressing Father Bear and then asking him a question. Mother Bear is asking both questions of Father Bear.<br><br>The white space on this page indicates that two different characters are speaking. Father Bear's speech is separated by *said Father Bear.* |

The last few pages use language structures similar to what is found on page 9.

*Needs of this group of readers in relation to the demands of the text:*

**Fluency**: Caroline and Michelle read in two- and three-word phrases, but there is no evidence of them reading longer phrases. Fluency has recently improved for the two girls since they stopped reading with their finger. Peter still reads word by word and without expression, even though he does not point to each word as he reads. Daniel is fluent. The singsong nature on page 7 and the dialogue in this text will support all of them to read in longer phrases and will help Peter use more expression. Rehearsing page 7 will model reading in groups of words and reading with expression.

**Dialogue**: Caroline will probably need support with the dialogue. She has been reading books where characters say one line of dialogue at a time. She has read simple direct questions such as "Where are you?" and "Where is the ball?" Direct address is a new type of dialogue. The students don't need to know what it is called, but they do need to know that it means the character is calling for one's attention before speaking ("Baby Bear, where are you?") This happens on three different pages in the book, so if Caroline gets support on one page, ideally she'll be able to transfer her skill to the other two pages independently.

*What to leave for reading work:*

The possessives on page 5 should not be challenging if students understand the meaning—that each character has a basket to collect blackberries. Adding an *s* to show possession is part of oral language these students control. It will be worth noting how the readers handle the phrase *Mother Bear's blackberries*; They may read it easily, or they may reread after they have made an error (e.g., "Mother Bear blackberries" for "Mother Bear's blackberries").

| **Plans for Book Introduction of *Blackberries* (see Figure 5.2 for what Kath wrote in her plans)** |
| --- |
| Notes for meaning statement: The Bear family went to look for blackberries and two things happened. See these baskets? Mother Bear and Father Bear wanted to carry them home full of blackberries, maybe make a pie or save them for the winter. But guess who didn't want to wait? (*Discuss.*) Then a serious thing happens—his parents lose track of him. Take a look and stop on page 9. |
| Language structures/sentence complexity:<br>p. 7: Baby Bear was singing a little song (rehearse). Use the picture to support the fact that Baby Bear is talking to himself.<br>p. 9: Explain that two bits of dialogue are separated by white space.<br>Explain the comma. Rehearse the second sentence: "Father Bear, is Baby Bear with you?" |
| Launch: As you read, think about how everyone feels as they go out to find blackberries. (This will support Peter with fluency when he reads the dialogue.) |

Figure 5.2

KATH'S PLANNING NOTES FOR *BLUEBERRIES*

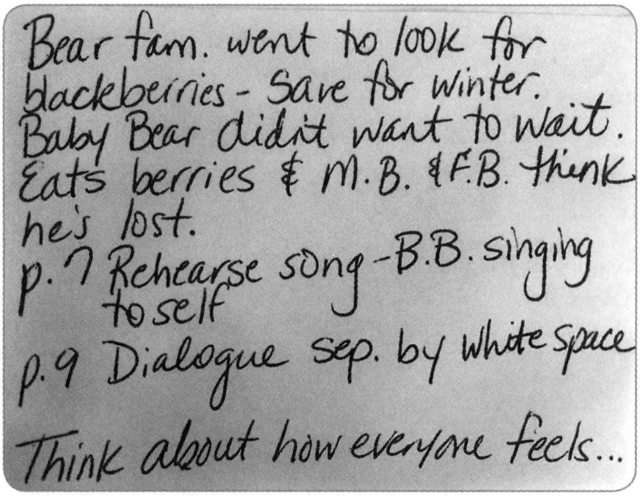
Bear fam. went to look for
blackberries - Save for winter.
Baby Bear didn't want to wait.
Eats berries & M.B. & F.B. think
he's lost.
p. 7 Rehearse song - B.B. singing
to self
p. 9 Dialogue sep. by white space
Think about how everyone feels...

Keep in mind that this is a plan, and a plan is a guide, not necessarily a script. It only represents your thinking before starting to work with students. During the actual interaction, the plan becomes a natural conversation as teacher and children respond to each other. As you read through this introduction, notice how Kath provided support for the students to access language structures and how the support affected meaning-making. You may also notice the on-the-spot changes Kath made to address students' needs while maintaining the flow and pace of the introduction.

| MS. FAY | You've read *Father Bear Goes Fishing*, right? This is another story about the Bear family. In this story they went to look for some blackberries. And when they went to look for blackberries, there were so many, and you know what? |
|---|---|
| CAROLINE | Baby Bear wants to eat them. |
| MICHELL | Lots of them! |
| MS. FAY | Yes he did! But Mother Bear and Father Bear wanted to take them home, so they had these baskets to put them in, but Baby Bear did not have the patience. Take a look and see if you can find the page where he eats them. (*Hands the book to the students.*) |
| CAROLINE | (*Flips to another page.*) He's eating a lot. |
| MS. FAY | And you know what else happens in this story? Something serious. He kind of gets lost; his parents can't find him. |
| CAROLINE | Yeah, he's so little that he's sitting and they're just over on the other side and saying, "Oh no, where's the baby?" |
| MS. FAY | Yeah, they're worried because they can't see him; he's kind of hiding in these bushes. Do you think he knows where his parents are? |
| DANIE | No. He's just eating. |
| PETER | Yeah, he's stuffing his face! |
| MS. FAY | I want to show you two things about this book. On this page where he's eating all the blackberries, he kind of sings a little song. It goes like this: "Blackberries, blackberries, I like blackberries." |
| ALL | "Blackberries, blackberries, I like blackberries." (*Caroline replaces* like *with* love.) |
| MS. FAY | It says *like.* "*I like blackberries.*" Let's say it again. Check it and see if it looks right. You see the *k*? (*Models running finger under the word* like.) |

| CAROLINE | (*Runs her finger under the word. Nods.*) Like. |
|---|---|
| ALL | *"Blackberries, blackberries, I like blackberries."* |
| MS. FAY | Also, I want to show you something on page 9. Do you see how worried Father Bear and Mother Bear look? They don't know where Baby Bear is! |
| CAROLINE | She looks like she's smiling. |
| MS. FAY | Oh, you're right, Mother Bear doesn't look worried! What about Father Bear? |
| MICHELLE | He's like, (*makes a worried face*). |
| MS. FAY | On this page, Mother Bear is talking to Father Bear. She said all of this (*frames sentence with fingers*). And down here, Father Bear said all this. See this space? They're showing you Mother Bear is talking here (*frames*) and Father Bear is talking here (*frames*). So right here it says, "'Where is Baby Bear?' said Mother Bear." And then, right here, do you see that comma? You have to take a little breath. Listen. (*Models reading the second sentence, demonstrating the pause at comma.*) Let's read that together. |
| ALL | "Father Bear, is Baby Bear with you?" |
| MS. FAY | Again. |
| ALL | "Father Bear, is Baby Bear with you?" |
| MS. FAY | That comma is telling you to pause just a bit, and that little pause helps us know that Mother Bear is getting Father Bear's attention. "Father Bear" (*pauses*). Try taking a little breath when you see other commas in the book. Okay, time to read it yourselves. When you read, think about how everyone was feeling. And what happened to all those blackberries! |
| MICHELLE | He ate them! |

The book introduction served its intended purpose. It provided students with enough support to successfully read, think, and talk about the book, while still leaving some reading work for them to do. For example, Peter (who had been reading mostly word by word with some two-word phrasing) read the phrases that had been rehearsed during the introduction fluently. He attempted some expression on the page where Mother Bear and Father Bear are talking with each other, which Kath reinforced: "You made her sound worried!" Her intention was to keep his mind on what was happening with the characters (focus on meaning). On the following page, Peter reread a sentence to sound more expressive without prompting. He still read word by word throughout much of the book, but he read in phrases when reading dialogue—a shift from what he had done while reading previous texts! Caroline, who substituted *love* for *like* during rehearsal in the introduction, was able to accurately read that part when she read the book, either because she looked at the end of the word (visual information) or because the phrase was familiar. After reading, the students talked about the Bear family's experiences and how they may have felt about thinking Baby Bear was lost and eating blackberries. Daniel and Michelle read this text easily.

We want our teaching to be generative so that what we teach today carries over into subsequent readings of a variety of texts. Sure, we may provide support to help students read a certain page in a book or have them rehearse a particular phrase, but that isn't the same as teaching them a generative strategy. In *Blackberries*, for example, rehearsing the little song on page 7 helped students read that page independently; the singsong cadence helped them remember the song and read it in phrases. It helped them with that one page in that one book. By contrast, showing students to pause at the comma (on page 9) is a strategic action that would help them as they read *Blackberries* and that they would be able to apply as they read future texts. We try to make interactions generative as often as possible. We *use* individual books to teach readers; we are not teaching kids to read individual books perfectly. Keep this in mind as you read the following tips for supporting readers with structure. You'll notice that the first part of the list helps students with the text at hand, whereas the second part has more generative value.

## SUPPORTING READERS WITH LANGUAGE AND SENTENCE STRUCTURE: A FEW TIPS

As you plan to support language structure and sentence complexity within the introduction, consider some of the following methods to help the text sound natural to students' ears:

*Use language in natural conversation.* Use some of the language of the text in conversation. During Kath's introduction of *Blackberries,* she used some of the language of the first page ("went to look for") in the meaning statement.

- *Rehearse phrases and sentences.* Children need to listen to you model sentences or phrases correctly and then have the chance to echo them. Sometimes the child who needs the most support doesn't join in the rehearsal, or mumbles through. Break the sentence into smaller chunks or give the group a chance to say it a few times. In the *Blackberries* example, Caroline needed to say it herself more than once to get the phrase right. Marie Clay reminds us why children need this practice with challenging language or pronunciations: "This allows the children to have a model of the language in their heads to support their reading of the text. It is not memorizing the lines of the book, but rather readying the mind and ear to grapple with the novelty" (1998, 174). This is especially helpful for English learners.

- *Introduce the text using the tense of the book.* Match the tense you use in the introduction to the tense of the text. This is particularly supportive of students reading the earliest-level texts. If the book is in past tense, use past tense ("Father Bear and Baby Bear went fishing and found something interesting"). If the book is written in present tense, as are many level A and B texts, use present tense in your introduction. For example, if the pattern is along the lines of "Dad can shop. Dad can cook . . . ," you might say, "This is a story about all the things Dad *can* do to make dinner. Let's look to see what Dad *can* do."

- *"Float" language during the first read.* This instructional move occurs after the book introduction. Use the new language structures in conversation as the readers turn the page or approach a tricky part. For example, if a page in the book starts with a prepositional phrase ("On Tuesday, Johnny went to . . ."), you could float the language ("Let's see where Johnny went *on Tuesday*") as the student turns the page and prepares to read it.

The preceding tips would certainly help children read specific texts. The following techniques are ways to support use of language structure in more generative ways. It's worth noting that some of these techniques could also be used while students are reading, or later in the lesson, during the teaching point.

- *Use generative terms.* Kath's language describing what to do when encountering a comma was generative; she even prompted students to try using it to pause on other pages in the book: "That comma is telling you to pause just a bit, and that little pause helps us know that Mother Bear is getting Father Bear's attention. Try taking a little breath when you see other commas in the book."

- *Place the phrase in and out of the text.* Explain the meaning of the phrase in the context of the book and give an example of the same phrase out of the book: "'The boy walked up to the tree.' This means the boy walked toward the tree. Let's try it. Watch me, I am going to walk up to the table. Now you walk up to the bookcase."

- *Use facilitative language to teach, prompt, or reinforce use of structure.* This may occur during the introduction, but is more likely to occur as the children read the book. For example, if a child says "I *goed* to the store" for "I *went* to the store," you might demonstrate: "I *goed* to the store makes sense but doesn't sound right. I *went* to the store makes sense and sounds right, too. You try it." Depending on the level of support you think the child needs, you might put more of the work on the student by prompting him or her to monitor and correct: "Try that again and make it sound right." Or, you might notice when a student uses language structure to effectively problem-solve while reading, so you reinforce the process: "You made it make sense and sound right, too."

The few, if any, supports offered for language structure are brief—a quick mention, demonstration, or rehearsal. They do not consume the bulk of the book introduction time. To maximize time with students, whatever supports we offer in the precious time we have must work toward making sense of the text and constructing possible deeper meanings of it.

The more familiar students become with complex language structures and complex sentences, the easier similar types of phrases will be to read. This is true for adults, too. Think of the books you read aloud to your class. Mo Willems's Elephant and Piggie books sound much smoother than *The BFG* (1982) by Roald Dahl. The BFG doesn't speak Standard English. Therefore, especially when reading aloud, we stumble a little and need to concentrate on how we sound, or we reread to make sure we understand the meaning behind what he is saying.

Fortunately, guided reading provides an opportunity for children to hear, try out, and eventually learn new language structures. Planning which phrases and sentences to draw out for students may seem a bit overwhelming at first, but the more we attend to the oral language of our students, the better we will become at deciding which structures we may need to support. Eventually, it will become commonplace to analyze guided reading texts with an ear for what might need to be highlighted. Quite often, our kids are our greatest teachers. Listen as they read. Take notes of phrases they stumble over. Take a second look at the words around their miscues. Notice their phrasing. These observations will inform how you introduce future texts.

*Our goal as teachers is to help children become active word solvers who can recognize words, take them apart or put them together, know what they mean, and connect them to other words—all directed toward reading and writing continuous texts.*

—FOUNTAS AND PINNELL (1998)

# CHAPTER
# 6

# Considering Words:
# IDENTIFICATION, DECODING, AND VOCABULARY DEVELOPMENT

Imagine a friend recommending a movie to you and starting out as follows: "This movie is about an ongoing war between two groups. There are a few words that are important for you to understand before watching: *galaxy, defector, knight,* and *resistance.* A *galaxy* is . . ." Would that draw you in and make you want to watch the movie? Would the interaction help you understand what you were about to see? Probably not. Sure, you might need to wrap your head around the meaning of those words to fully enjoy the experience of *Star Wars: The Force Awakens,* but the best way to learn about *resistance* or *defectors* is probably through the story itself. We get to know Finn and Rey's stories and motivations—why he defected and why she was so keen on supporting the Resistance—slowly, through their actions and reactions to others. Developing an understanding of key vocabulary within the context of greater meaning utilizes readers' natural-born tendencies to seek understanding through stories and ideas.

Each one of us has, at some point, begun a guided reading lesson by emphasizing words. While planning, we would preview the book, marking pages with potentially difficult vocabulary words or words that kids might struggle to solve. Then we would review those words in isolation with students before they read the book. Sometimes focusing on so many words made book introductions longer and longer, essentially becoming vocabulary introductions. Too often, the definitions we provided didn't help students learn what the words meant because they weren't attached to the context of the book. Telling students words that might be tricky to solve didn't allow them to use strategies to solve the words and often created a dependence on memory. ("You know this word. I already told you.") Our intentions, and those of teachers who have used similar practices, were positive. We anticipated words that kids might need to understand or might struggle with and "gave them" to the readers so they could successfully understand the book. Yet we were leading with individual words instead of leading with larger units of meaning. Leading with words unintentionally breaks down the wholeness of the text and its big ideas into isolated bits. It makes more sense to help kids enter the text thinking about meaning at greater levels. This way they can *use* the story to solve words or learn new vocabulary *while* they develop deeper understandings.

We intentionally placed this chapter toward the end of the book because often a teacher's tendency is to notice words first—which high-frequency words students need to recognize, which words might be hard to solve, which words might be difficult to understand. This is akin to looking at a piece of student writing and first noticing misspellings and lack of conventions because they are visually prevalent. Words, conventions, and spelling are important—we would never want to imply otherwise. Kids need to understand vocabulary and be able to automatically recognize or efficiently decode words in order to get to the author's intended message, and we need to teach them how to do this. However, our primary focus shouldn't be at the word level. Our goal is to shift a habit of mind so that we approach planning in a way that keeps the meaning of the text as the focus. Think back to the graphic of the hierarchy of written language we discussed in Chapter 1 (Figure 1.2). If you select an appropriate text and lead with meaning, the support at these lower levels of the hierarchy (letters, words, phrases) should be minimal. We'll work toward maintaining a meaning-driven approach to planning in this chapter by

- defining word solving through the lenses of word identification, decoding, and vocabulary development;

- considering ways teachers make decisions about which words to focus on during the book introduction; and

- exploring examples of how to embed support at the word level into larger meaningful contexts.

We've outlined a series of steps for planning book introductions in previous chapters: knowing students' strengths; analyzing the text; grounding the introduction in meaning; highlighting ways in which the book works; and rehearsing challenging language structures. The next step in planning a book introduction is making decisions about which words may need support. It has been our experience that when we follow the beginning steps, we significantly narrow the list of potentially challenging words. Thus, less is left for readers to grapple with at the individual word level.

To this end, we add to our ongoing planning process (step 4):

| |
|---|
| 1. Read the book for meaning. Think about what it's about and what it might really be about. Craft a meaning statement and a launching statement. |
| 2. Analyze how the book works (organizational structure and features). Plan how to support students (if necessary). |
| 3. Identify potentially challenging language structures and plan how to support students with them (if necessary). |
| 4. Determine words that may be difficult to solve (recognize or decode), or to understand (vocabulary), and plan how to support students with them (if necessary). |

Notice that the last three steps in this process caution us to use them only if necessary. This is key: weigh your students' strengths and needs against the potential challenges identified in steps 2–4 to determine what to introduce and what to leave for reading work.

Let's walk through step 4 as we continue to build habits of mind that help us plan effective introductions for students.

## WORD SOLVING: WORD IDENTIFICATION, DECODING, AND VOCABULARY DEVELOPMENT

Words are the building blocks that enable us to construct meaning as we read. To read proficiently, we must automatically identify and understand a great majority of the words we encounter in text, and flexibly apply a range of strategic actions to decode and understand words we are unsure of. Developing the capacity to efficiently solve words frees our attention to focus on larger units of meaning. Similarly, focusing on larger units of meaning while reading facilitates efficient word solving. Ideally, guided reading should provide just enough support for students to read at their instructional level with high levels of accuracy, fluency, and understanding while still having work to do that helps them grow in their capabilities. With this in mind, we make intentional decisions about whether and how we might support students with words during the introduction so that they are able to work through tricky parts while simultaneously maintaining their attention on meaning. Think of all we consider: the utility of the words, the students' ability to solve them independently, where we might leave opportunity for word solving, which words are crucial to understanding the story, and more. These decisions are not simple. And, depending upon the level of challenge, we vary the levels of support we provide in attending to print at the word level (Figure 6.1).

Figure 6.1
LEVELS OF SUPPORT

| Least amount of support | Leave most "tricky" words for reading work and observe how students attempt to solve them. |
|---|---|
| Moderate support | Predict and locate a few words. Mention some words by planting them in students' ears during the introduction. |
| Highest amount of support | Highlight one to three words, linking them with meaning whenever possible. Demonstrate how to solve one or a few words. |

To clarify, let's explore three different areas of word solving in greater depth, with excerpts of introductions that support each one.

## Word Identification

We refer to words that readers know automatically (without working to figure them out) as *sight words*. Sight words often consist of high-frequency words, and the term is expanded to include words that are meaningful and known to the individual reader. Some of the first sight words many children learn are their names, *no*, *STOP*, *Mom*, and *I*. They learn that each time they encounter these words, they say the same thing. ("*STOP* on the sign at the end of my street means the same as *stop* when my teacher writes it on the bathroom entry sign in the classroom.") The more readers read, the more sight words they add to their repertoire. Expanding their core of automatically identifiable words provides readers with more anchors to monitor their reading and propels the momentum of their reading forward. In other words, readers use their known words to read language in meaningful chunks or phrases instead of developing the theory that reading is about "figuring out this word, then the next word, then the next word."

At times, we may choose to have students locate a known sight word in early-level texts to teach them *how to attend to and search print* and develop automaticity if the word is newly acquired or partially known. ("Look, here is a word you know, *Mom*. When your finger points to *Mom*, you say *Mom*.") This teaching move supports students in using the known word to monitor their voice-to-print matching.

At other times, we may decide to use a procedure known as "predict and locate" to draw attention to a word that is not easily decodable or supported by meaning in the picture (*they, look, said*), especially if the word has high utility for the students' reading.

| Teacher | Say the word *said*. |
| --- | --- |
| Students | *Said.* |
| Teacher | What letter would you expect to see at the beginning of the word *said*? |
| Students | *S.* |
| Teacher | Find the word *said* and run your finger under it to see if you're right. |
| Students | (*Find* said *and run their finger under it as they look closely and say it slowly.*) |
| Teacher | Were you right? How do you know? |

Students are guided to do a lot with this procedure: attend to sound-letter correlation as they say the word and anticipate the letter they would see at the beginning, search print to locate the word, and closely attend to the visual information (letters) in the word as they run their finger under it, say it slowly, and check the sounds against the letters they see. Though it doesn't guarantee the children will read the word accurately when they encounter it again in text, this procedure at least readies their mind with a possibility and often leads to faster problem solving if not automatic recognition.

The following example shows one possibility of how drawing attention to high-frequency words during the introduction supports readers who are beginning to monitor with them.

**Planning Book Introductions: Supporting Word Identification**

### Teacher's Thoughts

*Balloons* (Dickey 1999) is a level B text. Each page shows a girl and her dog with a different color balloon. There are two lines of text on each page to describe what color balloon the girl and her dog like. The pages begin with either "I like" or "The dog likes." The demands of this book are such that to read it accurately, readers need to attend to the first word on each page because it varies from one page to the next. They also need to look at the picture (and possibly use the first letter) to determine the color of the balloon. Readers at this level mostly attend to the first part of words and will not likely notice the *s* at the end of *likes*, yet will read it correctly if it matches their oral language. At this level, if students do substitute *like* for *likes*, it will probably be ignored so that focus can remain on monitoring the variation of the way sentences start with the high-frequency words *I* or *The*. Planting the word *likes* through conversation and locating the words *I* and *The* would likely be the best way to support students with word identification.

### Excerpt of Introduction: Supporting Word Identification

Meaning statement: In this story, the little girl tells us about the different colored balloons that she likes. Her dog also likes colored balloons, but doesn't know how to play with them safely. What do you think might happen when he tries to play with the balloons? (*Discuss.*)

Supporting word identification—high-frequency words: Let me show you how this book works. On every page, the girl tells us which color balloon she likes and which color balloon the dog likes. You know the word *I*. Can you find it on this page? Sometimes the girl starts with what she likes: "I like red balloons." And sometimes she tells about the dog first: "The dog likes red balloons." Let's find the word *The*. (Writes *The* on whiteboard.) That's one of the tricks of this book. You have to notice which one she tells us about first: "The dog likes" or "I like." And you have to pay attention to the balloon colors! Let's read this first page together. Point to each word with your finger.

Launch: As you read, think about what the dog might like to do with the balloons!

This excerpt goes well beyond supporting students with word identification by drawing their attention to meaning, how the book works, language structure, and visual information. By letting readers know the book is about different colored balloons, the teacher conditions them to anticipate encountering a color word on each page, which narrows down the possibilities of what some of the unknown words may be, especially when students search the picture (meaning). By using some of the language structures in conversation, the teacher tunes students' ears to what would sound right (language structure). And by having them locate the words *I* and *The,* they help them learn what to attend to and where to look (visual) in the context of how the book works. These moves work together to limit the amount of time and attention the teacher spends on isolated words. Instead, it enables readers to think about the story as they read and better prepares them to talk about the book after they've read it.

## Decoding

Proficient readers have numerous ways to flexibly solve (decode) unknown words. A beginning reader may attempt to solve a word by using the first letter, such as *w* in *went.* ("The cat *went* in the kitchen.") They may also check to make sure their attempt makes sense and sounds grammatically correct. But this same reader may not yet know how to search the end of the word (*went* versus *was*) to confirm the attempt or monitor and correct the error. In more sophisticated texts, readers will need to use other strategies to solve words:

- use word parts to solve words (*st-uck*);

- break a word into syllables (*rib-bon*), or

- use what is known about one word to figure out another word (*for, wore*).

Of course, this list represents only a sampling, and strategies can vary, depending on your students and the levels of texts they're working on. As texts become more complex, the demands for word solving become more sophisticated. To learn more about what readers need to be able to do at particular text levels, we highly recommend studying the Guided Reading portion of *Literacy Continuum: A Tool for Assessment, Planning, and Teaching, Grades PreK–8* (Fountas and Pinnell 2017a), particularly the sections on solving words and planning for word work at each level.

We encourage you to remain tentative after planning. Even if your initial hunch is that students need very little support to decode the text, you may find yourself adjusting once the kids start reading, jumping in during that first read to provide meaning context or prompting a student to use a specific word-solving strategy. If you've provided moderate support by planting a word in the readers' ears during the introduction, they might breeze through that section, reading it accurately and with confidence. Did it help that you floated the word in conversation? Probably. Even if readers don't breeze through a word you mentioned, that interaction may still help them with their word solving. For example, readers who are working to use the sounds of letters and word parts to solve a word (*h-unt*) do more than simply pronounce it. Once they solve (or while solving) the word, readers check their attempt ("*Hunt,* is that right?") against words that they have spoken or heard. ("'The cat went off to'—*find*? No, *h-unt*. Oh! 'The cat went off to *hunt* the mouse.'") In this example, the reader did the work of solving the word, and may have been successful because the teacher provided a scaffold by generating an idea of a possibility. Think of a cartoon with thought bubbles above the reader's head, each with a possibility of what the cat may have gone off to do—*hide, search, hunt, pounce, hit.* The bubbles pop one by one as the reader narrows down possibilities using visual information in conjunction with meaning and structure until all that remains is *hunt.*

Will there be times when students stumble over words we thought they'd know or be able to figure out? Yes. Will there be times when we draw students' attention to a word, and then they surprise us by already knowing it during the introduction? Yes. While we use our observations and knowledge of students to plan ahead for how to support them (that's what this whole book is about!), we know that when it comes to the lesson itself, we follow what we notice in the moment as the kids are reading the book. We respond "on the run." We carefully observe and reflect on what our students do as word-solvers so that we can respond and adjust our teaching during the lesson or in future lessons.

What follows is an example of a book introduction plan that demonstrates a teacher highlighting a couple of words that may need to be solved during the book introduction for a group of students reading level E texts.

**Planning a Book Introduction: Supporting Decoding**

**Teacher's Notes**

*Dogs or Cats?* (Dufresne 2015a) is a level E text that compares the two animals of the title. It explores how they are trained, how they like to play, what they are good at—all to answer the question of why people like one animal more than the other. The last page of the book is a two-page spread that summarizes a few differences such as "Cats like to be alone" and "Dogs like to be with people" (15). Instead of headings, the book sometimes asks a question, such as "Why do people like dogs?" Students might benefit from rehearsing one of the questions or attending to the organizational format since it varies from other informational texts they've read. These readers are beginning to take apart compound words and use the parts to solve the larger word. This text has several compound words the students should be able to solve independently because they know a part or parts of the word (can-*not*, out-*side*). Many words are supported with meaning through the picture (*bathroom*) so there's no need to draw attention to them. The word *themselves* is also used in the text. There is a possibility that students may know the part *them* but may not be able to use it to figure out the word *themselves*. In this case, it makes sense to use that word to further demonstrate and reinforce the work of breaking apart compound words to solve them.

Even though readers will likely be able to decode small words like *sit* and *stay*, they might be unfamiliar with the words used in a phrase about dog tricks. If the teacher floats the phrase *sit and stay* in the air, it might become familiar enough to help them solve it.

**Excerpt of Introduction: Supporting Decoding**

<u>Meaning statement and how the book works:</u> This book is called *Dogs or Cats?* It compares dogs and cats, maybe for someone who is deciding which animal to have as a pet. Taking care of a dog is different from taking care of a cat! Which would you prefer to have, a dog or a cat? Why? (*Discuss.*) Let me show you how this book works. Whenever the author tells you something about a dog, like how it runs, she will tell you how a cat runs on the next page to compare how it is the same or how it is different. Let's look at page 4. On this page, it says that you can train a dog to do tricks, like sit and stay. Then, on this next page, it tells you that it is hard to train a cat to do those tricks. Take a look and see what else we might learn about dogs and cats. (*Kids flip through book and discuss.*)

<u>Supporting decoding</u>: Let's look at page 7. On this page, the author tells us whether the animals like to be with people or not. (*Discuss.*) Some cats like to be alone, or by *themselves.* Let's clap that word, *themselves.* Use your finger to look at the parts *them-selves.* Now let's read the whole sentence together.

Launch: Go ahead and read *Dogs or Cats?* See what it makes you think about wanting to have one or the other as a pet.

As in the previous example, some of the support for word solving was offered in the context of greater meaning while little work was done with words in isolation. Clapping the parts and putting their fingers in to break the word apart are behaviors that students can generatively apply to other words that work in a similar way. The teacher intentionally kept this interaction brief to avoid detracting from the overall meaning of the text. It might have been tempting to jump into a more in-depth word study lesson on compound words at this point, but she knew that it would be more effective to keep the focus on meaning before the reading. She could return to the principle of solving compound words during the teaching portion or even the word work portion of the lesson, after the students have read and discussed the text.

### A Note About Names and Titles

Characters' names can vary from common and easy to read (Sam) to unique and complex (Anastasia). As mentioned before, we consider the utility of words when we plan which to attend to and at what level of support, and which to leave for reading work. As a general rule, it is not beneficial to leave characters' names and the title of the book for reading work. Instead, we use the characters' names throughout the introduction and just tell students the name if they get stuck on it as they read: "Her name is Anastasia." Similarly, to keep students' initial interaction with the book successful, we state the title during the introduction and tell it to students again if they begin to read and struggle through it.

## Vocabulary

Our work with literacy learners requires us to support them in consistently acquiring new vocabulary as well as becoming flexible with multiple meanings of words they are familiar with. We provide them opportunities to use what's in the text (illustrations, words) and within themselves (background knowledge, oral language structures) to make meaning in the book they are reading today as well as in the books they will read in the future.

Let's return to the *Star Wars* example from the beginning of the chapter for a moment to consider supporting students with specific vocabulary. Imagine this introduction: "This is a story about a war between good and evil. The evil side, the First Order, wants power; it wants to control the galaxy. The good characters are fighting against the First Order so they can live freely and make their own decisions. They call themselves The Resistance. One main character, Finn, was born into the evil side and grew up working for them. Very early on, he defects—or leaves—the First Order. It's interesting to think why he decided to leave, especially since he grew up working there. Throughout the story, you may wonder why the characters act the way they do. Some of the characters are sure of themselves while others struggle with deciding how they want to live and work."

Contrary to the introduction at the beginning of the chapter, this one leads with meaning. The moviegoer has a sense that the word *resistance* means fighting against something, that the word *defector* means someone who leaves, and how those words fit into the story. Knowing a little about the story strengthens the understanding of those words and aids in understanding others. This introduction goes beyond simply planting vocabulary and gives moviegoers something to hang on to as they watch and consider the ways so many of the characters struggle with what to do. Although a strong introduction was provided, the moviegoer still needs to do a lot of work to connect the plotlines and keep track of the characters while considering some of the big ideas.

Teaching is decision making. When planning a book introduction, the teacher decides how much scaffolding to provide so that two things happen: the students construct the meaning of the text *and* the students grapple with some novelty, something new they are learning. All children, native and second language learners alike, are learning and developing their English vocabulary and the structures of language (turns of phrase, complex tenses), but each member of a guided reading group could be at a different stage. Our job is to determine, to the best of our ability, the capacity readers have to use context to understand the meaning of a word, phrase, sentence, or complete text.

Beck, McKeown, and Kucan (2002) write about a three-tier model (Figure 6.2) that provides guidance for us when considering which vocabulary words might need our focus.

Figure 6.2
THREE-TIER MODEL FOR VOCABULARY WORDS

| Tier 1 | Basic words that are simple and primarily learned without instruction. | mom , baby, look |
|---|---|---|
| Tier 2 | Words that are higher in frequency for mature language users, can often be found in written text, but are not as common in everyday language. Instruction on these words in the context of text is most effective. | replied, fierce, enormous |
| Tier 3 | Words that are not as frequently encountered, are limited to specific disciplines, and are best learned when needed in a content area. | circumference, predator, peninsula |

This research helps us understand how to categorize words as we make decisions about which words are worthy of attention in a book introduction. Abundant opportunities to speak, read, and write support students as they continue to add to their bank of words. And while Tier 2 and 3 words are more sophisticated, not all Tier 2 and Tier 3 words are equally important. With that in mind, we offer a few questions to guide decisions about which words to include in the introduction.

1. Consider the word's mileage. Will knowing this word add to the students' vocabulary in meaningful ways? Can this word be used in many contexts and situations?

2. How does the word relate to other words that students are learning? Will knowing this word support the understanding of other words and concepts?

3. Will knowing this word help with the major understanding of the text? Is knowing this word necessary to comprehend large chunks of the text or bigger ideas?

Let's consider how this plays out through an example with a level I fiction text.

**Planning a Book Introduction: Supporting Vocabulary Development**

**Teacher's Thoughts About the Text**

The level I book *Misa Learns to Ride* (Sanders 2004) is about a girl who overcomes her fear of riding her horse. There are multiple big ideas or themes readers might consider: things that appear daunting at first might not end up being that scary, for example, or tackling fears slowly may make it easier to approach a challenging situation. This story follows a common narrative story structure. The problem is introduced and is gradually resolved over a series of events; it is not a new text structure for this level. In this text, the sentence structures are common and most of the words are familiar. Readers at this level should be able to solve words like *year*, *rider*, and *helmet* and will most likely already know the meaning of those words or be able to easily infer them from context. In addition to the character names (Misa, Bella), the words *bridle*, *saddle*, and *paddock* might be new for the readers unless they have extensive experience riding horses. Of these, *paddock* is used five times in the text. Because *bridle* and *saddle* are used only once, we are inclined to leave those words out of the introduction to see how the children solve those words during the reading and to give them opportunities to infer meaning from context. There are multiple places in the text where students will need to think about the setting and what is happening as Misa is riding her horse, so we would intentionally plan to highlight the meaning of the word *paddock*, because it relates to where a majority of the story takes place. We might even have the students break the word apart (*pad-dock*) to reinforce a word-solving behavior that serves the students in problem solving not just on this word but also with other words, and in other books.

**Excerpt of Introduction: Supporting Vocabulary Development**

Meaning statement: Just as the title mentions, this story is about how Misa learns to ride a horse. But it isn't easy for her. She is very afraid. Have you ever been afraid to do something that you really wanted to do? (*Discuss.*) Thinking about how you felt will help you understand Misa's challenge, too.

Supporting vocabulary development: Misa and her horse will practice riding here in the *paddock*. A paddock is a small, enclosed area where the horses can run. (*Point to picture.*) Let's take a look at the word *paddock*. You can break it into parts. Try it. Look at the first part, *pad-*. Now look at and say the next part, *-dock*. Sometimes it helps to break longer words into smaller parts.

Launch: As you read, think about how Misa is changing as she learns to ride the horse.

In this example, the teacher told the students what the word *paddock* meant, used it in context, and pointed out additional meaning information in the picture. While defining a word in context is one way to support students with new vocabulary during the introduction, there are multiple other ways you might also succinctly approach it:

- *Use a known word part (affixes, base word):* "This section tells us a lot about recycling. If you know *re-* means to do again, and *cycle* is a process something goes through, then what might *recycle* mean? Using what you know about word parts can help you think about what new words mean."

- *Refer to resource tools such as a glossary:* "The author of this book included a glossary to help us learn what some of the important words mean. If you can't figure out what one of the words in bold print means, you can check the glossary in the back to see how the author defines it."

- *Point out when the author uses a synonym or defines a word within the text (often set off by commas):* "Sometimes an author defines a word right after he uses it in the sentence *(read example)*. Did you notice how he used commas to let us know he was telling us what the word meant?"

- *Infer word meaning based on context:* "Read the whole sentence and then think, 'What might that new word mean?' Try that synonym in the sentence. Does it make sense with what is happening in this part of the story?"

- *Link to a known concept:* "Think about what you know about [known concept] and ask, how might [new word] be connected?"

## PULLING IT ALL TOGETHER

Let's peek inside Kath's decision-making process as she determined which words to attend to during the introduction of a nonfiction text to a group of second graders. You can find what she wrote down for her plan in Figure 6.3.

---

**Teacher's Thoughts About the Vocabulary Demands of the Text**

The level M nonfiction book *Bats* (Russell-Arnot 1999) has several vocabulary words highlighted in bold print: *nocturnal, fruit bats, vampire bats, hibernation, nursing colony,* and *migration.* Kath needed to decide which would likely have the most instructional value. One possibility would be to highlight the word *nocturnal.* Three of the students were very knowledgeable about animals and probably knew what *nocturnal* meant. Drawing attention to this word, though, might expand students' knowledge by helping them see how being nocturnal affects how a bat lives, a bigger idea of the text. Another possibility could be to draw attention to the word *hibernation,* but since it is a large part of the science learning students have done in the primary grades, highlighting it is probably not necessary. *Nursing colony* is defined in the sentence and illustrated in the picture, so Kath decided to leave that for readers to sort out independently. *Migration* is potentially a new concept for these students. Because it is used in other contexts and conversations about animal life, it might be a word with some mileage. For this text, however, she decided not to include it in the introduction because the bulk of the ideas don't really relate to the concept of migration. Two of the other highlighted words (*fruit bats* and *vampire bats*) are merely types of bats. Their meaning could be derived from context and illustrations and would be of little instructional value for students to attend to during the introduction. Based on this analysis, it made the most sense to draw attention to the word *nocturnal* because it would affect how the readers understood multiple sections of the text—what bats eat, where they live, and how they care for babies.

In addition to the keywords noted in bold print, Kath noticed the almost poetic way the author described bats' wings with words like *stretchy.* She decided to briefly point out to students that the author took a word they knew (*stretch*) and added the ending *-y* to make *stretchy,* changing it from a verb to an adjective.

---

Figure 6.3
KATH'S PLAN NOTES FOR *BATS*

Now let's listen in to how Kath's plan plays out as she introduces *Bats*.

| MS. FAY | What do you think or know about bats? |
|---|---|
| CHRISTOPHER | Hmm. |
| NOAH | Bats are awesome. They're nocturnal. |
| MS. FAY | What else do you think? |
| SERENA | That they can sense anything. When they hear a sound, they just go right to it. |
| NOAH | Oh yeah, echolocation. |
| MS. FAY | What do you mean, "sense it"? |
| SERENA, NOAH, CHRISTOPHER | *(Three students talking at once)*<br>They can—<br>It's echolocation.<br>Yeah, and they're the only mammal— |
| MS. FAY | Let's let Serena start us off, and when you hear her finish talking, someone else can add on. |
| SERENA | It's like they—'cause, like, they—if they feel it move, they feel it coming to them. And maybe they think it's their food, so they go and check. |
| MS. FAY | Did you want to add to that? |
| NOAH | That's called echolocation. |
| CHRISTOPHER | And they are the only mammals that can fly. |
| MS. FAY | You guys know a lot about bats. Have any of you ever seen a bat, in real life? |
| CAMILA | At my pool there was one that flew across. |
| MICHELLE | Was it dark? |
| CAMILA | It was 7:30. They're nocturnal. |
| MS. FAY | *(To others)* Have you ever seen one? *(Kids shake their heads.)* We would most likely see them at night, right? Because they are awake at night and sleep during the day. When I first started learning about bats, they kind of creeped me out a little bit, maybe because of movies. Bats are in a lot of scary movies, maybe because they come out in the dark. But I discovered they actually have a lot in common with hamsters and dogs and even people. They aren't so scary! |
| MICHELLE | They look creepy in the picture because they have wings and they are like *(motions with arms)*, "Ooooh." |

| MS. FAY | Take a look at a few pages for some of the things you'll learn about bats in this book. (*Kids peruse quietly for a moment.*) |
|---|---|
| NOAH | They like to sleep together in caves. |
| MS. FAY | How they sleep. Camila said something about how they were nocturnal. What do you all know about being nocturnal? |
| MICHELLE | That they sleep in the day. Ooh, look! (*Points to the page where vampire bat is licking blood from another animal and reads.*) "What do vampire bats feed on?" |
| CHRISTOPHER, MICHELLE | Blood! (*Laughter.*) |
| MS. FAY | Everyone turn to page 7. I'm glad you noticed that. Look at the bottom. You see how that question is in a text box shaded in green and it has an arrow. If you flip to that next page, they'll answer that question. You can guess, "Blood, am I right?" Hmm, let's see. Now let's read that next green part. (*Chorally read*) "Vampire bats feed on animal blood." |
| CAMILA | That's what it looked like at my pool. (*Points to picture on page 8.*) |
| MS. FAY | Wow, that many. You saw that many? |
| NOAH | There was a swarm. Once I saw a vampire bat at my other school. |
| MS. FAY | I don't know that vampire bats live around here. When you read, check the map at the end of the book that tells where the different types of bats live. See what you think. |
| MICHELLE | Not all bats live in caves. |
| NOAH | Wait. Does it say that? |
| MS. FAY | What page is that? Let's all look at page 10 to see what Michelle is talking about. These two pages are about bat homes. So when you get to this page, you'll need to use the pictures and the words on these pages to think about where bats live. Thanks, Michelle. |
| MICHELLE | It's this kind that doesn't live in caves, I think (*points to picture*). |

**MS. FAY**

Great. Let's check back in after we read. Now please turn to page 2. At the top of page 2 it says, "What are bats?" It tells what you already know, that bats are nocturnal. But let's look at that word. Can you find the part that says *noc*? *Noc-turn-al*. Part of that word actually means "night" in another language. Want to read along with me? (*Reads that part.*)

Let me show you one more page. Turn to page 4. On this page the author is describing the wings. Listen to how she writes it. It kind of sounds like a poem: "The wings of bats look like hands with long fingers. Thin, soft, stretchy skin joins their long fingers together." Say that part with me, "Thin, soft, stretchy skin." I'll say it and you all repeat. (*Students repeat.*) Find the word *stretchy*. You guys know the word *stretch* (*motions*). The author added *-y* and turned it into a describing word. It's the type of skin that can be stretched. You could do that with other words, too, like *squeak*. The word *squeak* becomes—yes, *squeaky*. A squeaky toy.

All right, time to read. As you read, you might think about how being nocturnal affects the way bats live or what they eat. Because they are nocturnal, they may not eat the way we eat or they may not sleep the way other animals sleep. Enjoy!

The words we highlight should be important enough that, without introduction, the students might struggle to construct meaning, so Kath had planned to bring up the word *nocturnal*. As it turned out, not one, but two students mentioned it without prompting! (One of these students wasn't one she expected to know about the concept.) She decided to reiterate the meaning of *nocturnal* within the conversation. ("We would most likely see them at night, right? Because they are awake at night and sleep during the day.") Later, she drew attention to the word, making sure the kids recognized it visually and alluding to the idea that they might find out how bats' lives are different because they are nocturnal, which set students up for some of the discussion they engaged in after they read.

Words are important. In making decisions about which words to support, meaning remains the driving force. Noel Jones provides a perfect comparison to remind us of this importance: "Using the metaphor of a streamlined train, meaning is the engine and pulls forward all the cars of the train. Meaning generates the purpose and the movement forward. Meaning also leads and motivates monitoring and problem solving. Meaning affects every aspect of reading, including identification of letters and words on the page" (2013, 7).

Unfortunately, we encounter too many students whose train engines are powered by an overreliance on words, leaving meaning chugging behind in the caboose. These are often the same students who have developed a theory that reading is about "getting all the words right" rather than about understanding and thinking. Besides being impractical, leading with words sends an unintended message that reading is primarily about memorizing or remembering what words mean or pronouncing them correctly.

You have the power to avoid or change that message. Use your book introduction to lead with what the book is about and *might really* be about. Notice the organizational structure of the book. Support challenging language structures and make wise decisions about words. Leave students with opportunities to do some solving on their own. Let students use the story to infer what some words might mean. Words are important and interesting. They allow us to access the explicit and implicit meanings of the text. As you make decisions about which to highlight, always do so in the context of meaning—the meaning of the sentence, the significance of the scene, or the connection to the big idea of the text, supporting students in using that meaning as the engine of their reading.

*Conversations are powerful sculptors.*
*They shape our identities, thoughts, beliefs,*
*and emotions.*
—ZWIERS AND CRAWFORD (2011)

## CHAPTER

# 7

# Thinking Together:
# EXTENDING MEANING THROUGH DISCUSSION

Chrisie's colleague Shele raved about the book *Fox* by Margaret Wild (2006). An avid book collector, Chrisie ordered it, sight unseen, based on the glowing recommendation. She tore into the box when it arrived, immediately read the highly anticipated book, and . . . wasn't exactly a huge fan. "This is a kids' book!?" thought Chrisie . "But it's so dark and depressing! I don't even know what happened at the end. Shele loved this?!" She set the book aside and didn't think about it for a while.

That year, *Fox* was used in several professional development sessions in our district, each time serving as the focal point of discussion, and Chrisie broadened her view. As others shared their thoughts, she considered different interpretations of the characters and events and thought more deeply about the crafting techniques the author, Margaret Wild, and illustrator, Ron Brooks, used. One colleague commented, "Magpie really redeemed herself at the end by returning to Dog." Chrisie thought, "Redeemed? I wasn't thinking about her like that. I originally thought Magpie was selfish; she left Dog when something better came along. Now that I think about it again, maybe Magpie realized that Dog was her true friend, motivating her to make the long, hard journey back to him." Another colleague brought up the recurring references to fire in phrases such as *scorches through the woodlands* and the contrast of the red-colored fox against a dismally colored background, and Chrisie began to pick up on some of the symbolism, leading her to a deeper appreciation for the beauty in this artfully crafted text. And, while no group could ever come to consensus about the ending, she marveled at the power cognitive dissonance had on her thinking as a reader. She realized, "Maybe I don't need a happy ending to enjoy a book after all." The opportunity to talk about *Fox* completely changed Chrisie's opinion of the book and kept her thinking about it days later. Without the chance to talk, to listen, to reconsider *Fox* with others, those ideas would have been lost.

How does Chrisie's story relate to our work with children? It's a reminder that engaging in an authentic discussion with others has the potential to foster, change, and deepen thinking. This is true regardless of whether the discussion occurs after reading a book independently, listening to a book read aloud, or reading a book during small-group work, such as guided reading. These conversations do two things: they allow the children to process what they have just read with others, and they provide teachers with insights into the children's developing thinking.

The book introduction and the discussion after reading are symbiotic. We sow the seeds for readers to construct meaning with a well-planned book introduction, and we end the lesson by giving them time to unearth their ideas through conversation. The guided reading environment should, as much as possible, support the kind of thinking we want kids to do as strong, independent readers. We don't wait until they are more mature readers to provide opportunities to actively engage with books and each other. Rather, we support thinking and talking from the earliest days of interacting with print. The effect of our work in analyzing texts and planning supportive book introductions is revealed as students read and as they talk afterward. Making time for the discussion is imperative. How you facilitate the talk is an art that we will unpack in this chapter as we explore

- the effect of discussion on meaning-making,

- how common pitfalls may affect students' theories of reading,

- what's worth talking about with texts,

- establishing routines and a culture of talk, and

- various hats teachers wear during text discussions.

## DISCUSSION DEEPENS UNDERSTANDING

If we think about our experiences as readers, we talk all the time to deepen our understanding of what we've read: we pause and comment while reading, or share our responses to what we have read with others afterward (though maybe not immediately). Through talk, we clarify, rephrase, synthesize, summarize, question, and infer. Yet we sometimes forget that talk has the very same effect on how young readers develop understandings about what they read. Often, especially with early readers, what gets emphasized in guided reading is developing strategic actions for word solving and establishing concepts about print. These areas are certainly foundational in learning to read, but if readers don't also comprehend the story or ideas in the text, then they aren't truly reading; they are merely word calling. Engaging students in conversations about the books they read allows them to do more of the thinking work that reading requires and makes the act of reading more enjoyable for all.

Talk can be an external representation of our internal thinking. In a sense, it makes much of the invisible (thinking) work of reading "visible." We observe students as they engage in discussion and interpret their remarks as evidence of thinking: students summarize what happened, draw upon personal experiences, put ideas together, and test out theories. It makes sense, then, that if we want to understand and develop the whole reader, we allot time for them to engage in discussion of what they've read. This is important for all readers, especially for English learners. The small-group format of guided reading provides a safe place for students to try out their ideas in discussions, with the support of the teacher as facilitator.

Talk can also be a vehicle for negotiating meaning. Consider how many times you engage in inner dialogue as you're making decisions ("Should I do this or that?") or consult a friend ("Can I talk something through with you?"). Facilitative conversations help us consider possibilities, weigh consequences, confirm hunches, and deepen thinking. Listening to and considering the ideas of others forces us to clarify and strengthen our thoughts or to change them as we gain additional perspectives. In similar ways, sharing our thinking invites others to listen, reconsider, and respond, and thus contributes to their understanding.

The discussion after a guided reading lesson should be an authentic and natural exchange of ideas. Why these parameters? Again, these are the types of readerly interactions proficient readers have after they read. We read a professional article and talk to colleagues about what we agree with or disagree with or how to incorporate ideas into our practice. We read a newspaper article and comment to our partner, critiquing the events and the actions of politicians here and across the globe. We read a novel and talk during our book clubs about the character's decisions, wondering why the author chose to make her behave in such extreme ways. Children shouldn't have to wait until they are adults to have these types of discussions. Literacy expert Regie Routman supports this idea by reminding us to "[r]espect children's rights as readers and allow them the same rights we have" (1996, 84). We believe in the power of respecting these rights by engaging children in authentic conversations about texts from the start.

Although some may wonder whether young children are capable of holding these types of discussions, we have found that with instruction and guidance they can. Let's listen to a group of first graders discussing *Birds* (2012) by Rose Lewis and notice how their ideas about the function of birds' body parts develop.

| | |
|---|---|
| **MS. ADAMS** | Before you started reading *Birds*, I asked you to think about what you were learning about the characteristics of birds. So, what's something you learned that was new or interesting to you? |
| **HALEY** | They have a tooth that cracks the egg open. |
| **DEVIN** | They have different kinds of feathers. |
| **MS. ADAMS** | Let's think more about that together. Turn to page 5. What did you notice about the information in the diagram? |
| **SAL** | Look at the feathers. They are see-through! |
| **DEVIN** | The ones on their body are short, and these ones (*pointing to the wings and tail*) are long. |
| **MS. ADAMS** | They are, aren't they? Tell us more about what you're thinking about that. |
| **SAL** | The long ones help them fly. |
| **HALEY** | Yeah, and the short ones are fluffy and warm. |
| **MS. ADAMS** | Hmm, I think you might be on to something. Turn back to page 3. The author told us that some birds can fly but others can't. Looking at the picture [seagull flying, penguin not flying], why do you think that might be? |
| **SAL** | They don't have any long feathers, so they can't lift up. |
| **DEVIN** | (*Looking closer at the picture.*) Do they have feathers on their wings? |
| **HALEY** | Yeah, the little ones, because to keep them warm there. |

| DEVIN | Penguins are fat, too. |
|---|---|
| MS. ADAMS | So even though all birds have feathers and wings, the types of feathers they have might be different. Their special feathers might help them do things, or keep them from doing things. It seems their beaks might be like that, too. What are you thinking? |
| DEVIN | (*Turning to pages 6 and 7.*) That one (*pointing to the hawk*) has a sharp one to get the animals. |
| MS. ADAMS | He has to kill his prey, or other smaller animals like rabbits and mice, for food, doesn't he? |
| SAL | And that one has a long one to go down and get the fish. |
| HALEY | Why is the duck's round? |
| MS. ADAMS | I'm not sure. But if the others' have a reason, I bet the duck's does, too. |
| DEVIN | To get his food. |
| MS. ADAMS | It probably does have something to do with that. So, what does all this make you think about birds now? |
| DEVIN | They all have wings and feathers and eggs, but different kinds of them. |
| MS. ADAMS | Ahh! In fact, many living things work like that. Animals and people, but even plants, too. Think about the different types of leaves trees have or how plants have stems and leaves but grow different fruit. Pretty cool, huh? |

In discussions such as the one above, thoughts are shared, questions are asked, ideas are inferred, and links are made to the text. Is there more that could be discussed? Absolutely. But the goal isn't to talk a book to exhaustion; rather it is to share, deepen, and sometimes reconsider an idea because we had the chance to mull it over with others. Thinking is the point of reading. From the teacher's point of view, guided reading provides an opportunity for students to successfully read and think about books with support and instruction. From the students' point of view, guided reading is joyful time with a book and, after reading it, a place for an authentic discussion of what they and others thought about it.

The first-grade discussion of *Birds* sounded similar to one that adults might have when discussing a nonfiction text. To facilitate, Ms. Adams's prompting was pointed yet open-ended. This gave students a chance to explore a line of thinking in more depth. For example, after Haley shared about the egg tooth,

Devin immediately followed by talking about feathers. If Ms. Adams had taken a backseat in the conversation, Sal may have jumped in with another interesting tidbit and the conversation may have ended up sounding more like a list of facts. Instead, Ms. Adams prompted the students to linger with Devin's idea about feathers for a bit when she said, "Let's think more about that together." This led to further conversation and ultimately a deeper understanding that various types of feathers or other body parts can help or hinder animals in different ways. Ms. Adams makes a conscious effort to engage her students in conversations like this day after day, which positively affects children's reading identities, sense of community, and overall comprehension. Her students begin to develop a theory that reading and talking about books like this helps them learn, is pleasurable, and is worthy of their time.

## COMMON PITFALLS AND UNINTENDED CONSEQUENCES

All students deserve opportunities to authentically discuss text. There are various factors, though, that sometimes get in the way. Some hindrances pertain to us, the teachers, over-managing instead of facilitating conversations. Others include school and classroom factors such as time management. In contrast to Ms. A.'s discussion with her students, consider how the following mock pitfall conversations about *Birds* might contribute to students developing ineffective theories of reading. Please note that we are not offering the labels below as a judgment, but rather to begin a professional dialogue on how we might improve discussions that draw out student thinking.

### The Endless Evaluation

High-stakes testing brings out a fear that if we don't frequently use testing language during instruction, we are doing a disservice to students by not providing tools essential to pass tests. In many commonly used assessments, for example, students are asked to fill in the blanks with missing words or to answer a battery of questions that address specific standards. In an effort to support students, teachers sometimes use the same types of questions during daily instruction. Imagine the outcome when teachers use these types of questions as the sole source for discussion about texts.

| T | What did we learn? Birds have wings, feathers, and? |
|---|---|
| S1 | Beaks. |
| T | Good job. What are the two reasons birds have feathers? |
| S2 | To fly and stay warm. |
| T | That's right. How do birds keep their eggs safe? |
| S3 | They fight off other animals. |
| T | True, but that's not what the book said. Who remembers what the book said about how birds keep their eggs safe?<br><br>(*Later in the conversation*) So what connections do you have to this book? |
| S1 | I saw a bird flying in the sky once. |
| S2 | I have a book about birds at home and it had different eggs, too. |
| S3 | I like to feed birds in the winter, too. |
| T | Great connections. |

This scenario follows the traditional initiate-response-evaluate (IRE) model. The teacher initiates, or poses a question. A student responds. The teacher then evaluates the student response and replies in a way that lets the student know whether he or she was right or wrong before proceeding, essentially turning the interaction into a verbal test. Are there times when it is helpful to confirm or refute a student response? Of course. We just want to be sure we don't set up a dynamic where we become a gatekeeper of questions and responses and lose the power of children responding to and learning from one another.

Just because something is used for assessment doesn't mean it is a best practice for instruction. Certainly, we must observe students and make notes of their strengths and needs to guide our planning and teaching; however, we don't use guided reading time to test them on the book. In her book *One Child at a Time*, Pat Johnson reminds us:

> *Keep in mind that guided reading is not a testing situation. It's instructional time with the student, time to teach and support readers. We don't prepare students for a writing prompt test by giving them constant writing prompts, but rather by developing strong writing workshops that include instruction*

*on writer's process, author's craft, and mechanics.
In the same way, we don't use guided reading
instructional time to practice for a benchmarking
test. We use instructional time to teach reading
strategies and behaviors that the child can use
on any text, even ones they encounter in a testing
situation. (2006, 130–131)*

If we constantly assess comprehension rather than teach for it, we inadvertently develop readers' theory that every "discussion" is a test and students need to either prove that they mastered the book or didn't. Kids are smart. They figure out pretty quickly when a teacher is looking for a specific response. Then they tune out, give up, or think responses are always either right or wrong. This negatively affects both the kids who constantly answer the questions correctly and those who disengage.

## The Retell and Regurgitate

Another popular way to assess text comprehension is to ask students to retell what they've read, thinking that if they can recap the book detail by detail, then they must understand it. This is often done without the ability to "cheat" by referring to the book.

| T | (*To the group*) Start at the beginning and tell me what the author said about birds in this book. |
|---|---|
| S1 | Some birds can fly and some can't. |
| T | Okay, but what did she say about birds before that? |
| S1 | Umm . . . (*reaches for his book*) |
| T | Keep your book closed. I want to see what you remember. Who can help him out? What did the author say first? |
| S2 | Birds have wings, and feathers, and beaks. |
| T | That's right. Then what did she say? |
| S2 | The feathers help them stay warm and, um, fly up in the sky? |
| T | Keep going—then what? |
| S2 | They have beaks that are different shapes. (*Retelling continues until students get to the end.*) |

Consider how you discuss books with friends and colleagues. We doubt any of you sit down and retell what you've read detail by detail. The goal isn't to prove to your friends that you read the book! You may concisely summarize all or part of the text to make or counter a point, but the true pleasure of reading and discussing what you've read comes from digging into the interesting information, characters' decisions and thoughts, or emotions that surfaced for you as you read. As you talk about these compelling components, you likely dip back into the text, using it as a resource to ground your thinking. Why should we expect anything less from our young readers? When we regularly ask readers to retell, students might develop an erroneous theory that reading is about memory—remembering all the details in order to regurgitate the text to the teacher.

## A Game of 20 Questions

Irene Fountas often says our conversations with students about books should be "conversations, not interrogations." Despite many teachers agreeing with this statement, another common pitfall is when the teacher showers students with questions, often in a round-robin format.

| T | (To student 1) What's something you learned about birds? |
|---|---|
| S1 | There's a lot of types of birds. |
| T | (To student 2) What's something you learned? |
| S2 | Some eggs are pointed. |
| T | (To student 3) How about you? |
| S3 | The babies have an egg tooth that breaks the shell open. |
| T | (To student 1) What did the book say about birds' feathers? |
| S1 | They help them fly. |
| T | (To student 2) What else did it say about birds' feathers? |
| S2 | They keep them warm. |

In this excerpt, there is no cross-talk that allows the students to linger with an idea for a bit or debate an idea with one another. Instead, every comment is filtered through the teacher. She poses a question, and a student responds. This teacher might think students "got the book" because each one was able to respond to what she asked. A similar interaction with a fiction text might be centered on questions related to elements of the story: "What was the problem? Who was in the story? What was the solution?" Responses only show evidence of literal understanding, as the questions ask students to recall details or facts that are explicitly stated in the text. Even if the teacher had asked some higher-level questions about *Birds*, the interaction would have remained fairly flat because the steady question format doesn't provide room to grow an idea. Students subjected to a diet of this type of interaction might become passive. Their theory of talking about texts might become, "Think fast, then say the first thing that comes to mind. If I answer correctly, I'm off the hook until the teacher makes her way back to me again."

## The Read and Move On

Let's face it: time is often our enemy. In a jam-packed day we might be tempted to forgo conversation in order to try to squeeze in another guided reading group or move on to the next component of our day. Or, we might simply forget to have the conversation because we are in a rush. After all, isn't it good enough that students have the chance to read a book at their instructional level? Not really. Students deserve the opportunity to talk about what they've read. We put a high priority on thinking and making meaning from text so we must insist on opportunities, even brief ones, to think together. When we don't, the end of a lesson might sound like this:

| T | *Birds* was a good book, wasn't it? |
|---|---|
| S | Yes. |
| T | Great reading. Tomorrow we will read _____. I think you'll like that one too. Now hurry back to your literacy station so I can meet with the next group! |

Skipping the discussion builds a theory that reading is mostly about saying the words on the page, then moving on, and not something they really have to engage with. Rushing to meet with more and more groups replaces quality with quantity. Even a two-minute conversation can be valuable. And if we are short on time one day, we can at least invite students to turn to a partner for a quick moment to process through their thoughts about the book.

These common pitfalls create what we refer to as "school reading" because they most often occur within the walls of school buildings and seldom occur elsewhere. If we turn reading during the school day into mere "school reading," we run the risk of raising students who develop negative theories (and often poor habits) of what reading is all about. One way to heed this caution is to check that what we're asking of kids in school reflects the everyday ways in which readers talk about books outside of school.

## WHAT'S WORTH TALKING ABOUT? INITIATING AND FACILITATING MEANINGFUL CONVERSATIONS

Now that we've established that talking about books is important to comprehension, it's worth exploring how to initiate and facilitate meaningful conversations, with two essential questions: "What's worth talking about?" and "How do we guide meaningful conversations?" We've found two effective methods for opening a meaningful discussion. The first is simple—ask an open-ended question and follow the lead of the group. The second circles back to the introduction and uses ideas posed in the launching statement as a springboard. Once we initiate the discussion, we use facilitative language as needed to keep the focus on areas of conversation that replicate what we, as proficient readers, talk about. To guide our thinking with this, we use a process of spying on ourselves as readers to ensure the authenticity of what we nudge our students to talk about.

### Open-Ended Question or Statement

It is good practice to begin conversations in as open-ended a way as possible so that the ideas your students have percolating in their minds while reading can be explored out loud. We might open the conversation by simply asking, "What are you thinking?" or "What are you thinking about [topic/ character]?"

One of the things we have been experimenting with is making statements instead of always asking questions. Instead of, "What are you thinking?" try, "I wonder what you're thinking about this book." You might also try referring to something a child lingered on while reading. "I noticed you giggling on this page." You can also restate something that happened in the story: "Chameleon searched and searched for his meal." Then, wait for the kids to respond. It may not happen the first time. You may need to model a bit so that they learn what you mean by those open invitations. Eventually they will become more actively engaged students who pose questions to each other or share ideas spontaneously.

## Link to the Launching Statement

In Chapter 3, we discussed launching students into their reading with a question or statement that invites them to consider the meaning of the text. It makes sense, then, to open the discussion after reading by returning to the launching statement with a related open-ended question or statement. In Figure 7.1, notice how the teacher links the discussion opening to the launching statement so that both interactions point students toward understanding.

Figure 7.1
LINKING THE LAUNCHING STATEMENT TO OPENING MOVES

| Title, Author, and Level | What's It About? | What Might It Really Be About? | Launching Statement from the Book Introduction | Possible Opening Moves for Discussion After Reading |
|---|---|---|---|---|
| *Dolphins and Porpoises*, Melvin and Gilda Berger, Level I | This book shares factual information about what dolphins and porpoises look like and how they live. | Although dolphins and porpoises share similarities, there are many characteristics that distinguish them from each other. | While reading, consider how dolphins and porpoises are similar to and different from each other. | What are you thinking about dolphins and porpoises now that you've read this book? How are they similar? Different? |
| *Cat Naps with Oliver*, Will Renton, Level D | Oliver finds a comfortable spot on the bed to take a nap, until Boomer decides he wants to take a nap in the same spot too. | Sometimes you just want quiet time and space to yourself.<br><br>It's nice to cuddle up with family.<br><br>You may be able to get what you want when you ask nicely. | Read and see what you think about why Boomer wants to sleep on the bed. | On the last page, Boomer said, "Purr! Purr! Purr!" I wonder what he's thinking.<br><br>Talk about how the characters feel at the end. |

*(continues)*

*(continued )*

| *Jaxson's Animals,* Michele Dufresne, Level A | Jaxson shows us all the stuffed animals he has that he likes, and one real animal (his pet dog, Boss) that he loves. | Toys are fun, but nothing beats the real thing.<br><br>Pets are great because they can play with you and love you back. | As you read, think about how much Jaxson likes all his different animals. | Which is Jaxson's favorite animal? Why? |
|---|---|---|---|---|

While linking back to the launching statement brings cohesion to the front and back ends of the reading, when we reflect on our own genuine conversations about texts, we rarely follow only one line of thinking. Instead, we tend to follow one idea for a while until we run out of meaningful things to say or until one line of thinking leads to another idea. With this in mind, we plan ways to open the conversation and then leave space for thinking that stands out to the readers, based on what they understand and perceive, rather than what we may have thought when we read and analyzed the book. We keep follow-up questions or statements in our back pockets to guide toward deeper thinking, and shape the discussion when necessary, using just enough to keep the conversation flowing without crossing the line of moving into "interrogation."

## Spying on Ourselves as Readers

To study authentic conversations that readers have, we look inward to "spy on ourselves as readers" and think about what we tend to find worthy of talking about. Chrisie and several groups of her colleagues recently read a short text and talked about it in small groups. As teachers talked, Chrisie transcribed what they said. Afterward, they studied the transcript for trends, and formed categories of what they talked about, as shared in the first column of Figures 7.2 and 7.3 (Focus of Conversation). Then, they asked, "If this is what we as proficient readers talk about, how might we promote similar authentic conversations amongst our students?" With this question in mind, they developed the second column of Figures 7.2 and 7.3 (How We Might Facilitate Conversations), which offers possible language to share our thinking, model how to think, and prompt thinking in others.

Figure 7.2
Discussion of Fiction/Narrative Text

| Focus of Conversation | How We Might Facilitate Conversations |
| --- | --- |
| Drawing upon background knowledge | • This reminds me of _____ , so it has me thinking that _____.<br><br>• Have any of you been in a similar situation? How do your experiences help you understand _____ better? |
| Character description | • When the character did _____ and said _____ , it made me think she was _____. What are you thinking about the character? What makes you think that?<br><br>• How would you describe the character? |
| Character motivation | • I'm thinking that he [action] because [rationale]. What are you thinking?<br><br>• Why do you think he did/said that? |
| Character's evolution | • I started to think differently about the character as I read across the story. How about you? What were you thinking?<br><br>• How do you think the character changed throughout the story?<br><br>• What did you notice about the character's actions and words at the end of the story compared with the beginning? |
| Turning point in the story/for the character | • I thought _____ was an important [action/event/realization], because it helped the character to _____.<br><br>• What are your hunches about what made the character change? |
| Resolution of the problem | • At first I thought the story was going to end with _____ , but I was happy to see _____. What do you think about how it ended?<br><br>• What do you think about how the story ended?<br><br>• What are you thinking about [character/problem] now? |

*(continues)*

*(continued )*

| | |
|---|---|
| Author's choice of language | • I loved how the author wrote _____. Those words really helped me [think/feel/see].<br><br>• What did you notice about the language/words the author chose? |
| Opinions of the text | • I really enjoyed/didn't enjoy this book because _____.<br><br>• What did you think of the story? |
| Questions and wonderings | • I'm still not sure about _____.<br><br>• What does this book leave you wondering about? |
| Big ideas and themes | • What I'm taking away from this book is _____.<br><br>• What do you think the author might want us to be thinking about?<br><br>• What might this book really be about? |
| Actions the reader wants to take | • Now that I've read this, it makes me think that I need to _____ in order to _____.<br><br>• How might we apply the messages of this book to our lives? |

Figure 7.3
DISCUSSION OF NONFICTION/EXPOSITORY TEXT

| Focus of Conversation | How We Might Facilitate Conversations |
|---|---|
| Interesting or surprising information | • I couldn't believe it when I read _____. I had always thought _____.<br><br>• What did you learn that was interesting or surprising to you? |
| New information and how it fits with what we previously thought | • Now that I've read this book, I'm thinking ___. What are you now thinking?<br><br>• How does what you read fit with what you were thinking before you read the book? |

| Drawing upon background knowledge or experiences | • I remember a time when I saw _____. It was very similar to how the author described ____, so I can see why _____.<br><br>• What does this book make you think of? How are you using what you know or have experienced to help you better understand [the topic]? |
|---|---|
| Big ideas and themes | • What I'm taking away from reading this book is _____.<br><br>• What might be the author's bigger message(s) to us about [topic]? |
| How the information is conveyed/organized | • Knowing this book is organized by _____ helped me to summarize the key points.<br><br>• What did you notice about how the author organized the book? How did that help you think about/understand what you read? |
| What we still wonder and want to know | • I still want to know _____ so I'm going to have to read more to find that out.<br><br>• What do you wish the author had included that you're still wondering about? |
| How we might use the information/take action because of what we read | • Now that I know this, I'm going to be sure to _____.<br><br>• What does this information leave you thinking about or wanting to do? |

After doing this work, it was apparent to Chrisie and her colleagues that what was worth talking about in narrative texts went far beyond a recap of the plot, and expository text sparked more than simply sharing a collection of facts. Readers shared what they found to be significant: new and interesting ideas, wonderings, criticism of the text, how the information gleaned affected their actions, and more.

The examples in Figures 7.2 and 7.3 are very helpful, yet these lists are by no means exhaustive or hierarchical. We include them to offer broad categories that might serve as tools for planning and facilitating discussions with students. After spying on themselves, one of Chrisie's colleagues admitted to being somewhat stuck in a rut by often asking students what they learned once they finished reading a nonfiction book. After this experience, she expanded her repertoire of possibilities for openers such as "You've just learned a lot about recycling from this book. What does it leave you thinking about or wanting to do?" Another teacher used the categories to design launching statements. She introduced a text with a character whose evolution was a driving force of the plot. Her launching statement was, "As you read, think about how the character changes throughout the story." After the students read, she circled back and began the discussion with, "Let's talk about the changes [character] went through."

## ESTABLISHING ROUTINES AND A CULTURE OF TALK

To establish a classroom environment that sings with collaboration, we must be adamant about fostering a culture of talk throughout our literacy block and throughout the day. Every school year begins by teaching this kind of talk during whole-group settings such as interactive read-aloud and morning meetings, and by meeting with students in small groups or partnerships. The focus in the partner and small-group work is on listening and talking with each other about texts. Within a few weeks, guided reading groups begin meeting and the practice of listening to one another, expanding on each other's lines of thinking, and deliberating ideas continues. When students are taught these routines, they come to expect that this is the way readers talk about texts. And they develop collaboration and conversation skills that support them well beyond talking about books.

We, once again, return to ourselves to note authentic talk routines and facilitation techniques. While Chrisie's colleagues spied on themselves as readers as they discussed texts, she also took note of the conventions of conversation that naturally took place. Bringing the unstated rules and routines they automatically and unknowingly followed to the surface helped determine several key areas to teach their students.

### Ways We Talk with Each Other and Develop Ideas

- Listen respectfully and purposefully.

- Take turns.

- Support ideas with evidence.

- Grow ideas together.

Children take on these rules and routines through experience and instruction. We model them explicitly, prompt for their use, reinforce attempts at applying them, and provide numerous opportunities to practice so that children learn to adopt conversational behaviors. Let's zoom in and explore each.

## Listen Respectfully and Purposefully

Listening is an element of active participation. We demonstrate active listening and communicate respect to others by making eye contact with them and holding our own thoughts until it is an appropriate time to respond. We nod our head or give slight verbal responses, like, "Mmm-hmm" to signify our attention. These behaviors show interest in and respect for what the speaker is saying.

Focused listening also helps us attend with purpose. As Maria Nichols shares, "Listening with intent involves letting the idea being heard into our brain, and actually engaging with it" (2006, 42). In this way, we absorb the speaker's message, consider it, and then respond in a manner that adds to the thinking or provides an alternative view, helping us to grow ideas with one another.

As adults, we often take these "unstated rules" of respectful listening and responding for granted. But we must remember that young children just learning to engage in these conversational exchanges may need explicit instruction and support in taking them on. Take a peek at a discussion to see how one teacher does just that.

| | |
|---|---|
| **MS. DAVIS** | (*Before the discussion starts*) As we talk about *Allie's Basketball Dream* (level K) today, let's make it a goal to really listen to one another. When you're listening, look at the person who is speaking. Take in what they are saying and ask, "What do I think about that?" This will help you understand what they are saying and help you decide if you want to add to or challenge it.<br><br>So, what are you guys thinking about Allie and her basketball dream? |
| **KAYLA** | (*Looking at Ms. D. as she speaks*) She went to a pro basketball game with her dad and she—she wanted to be just like them [the professional players] so she played basketball all the time but boys said she couldn't 'cause she's a girl. |

| MS. DAVIS | Push pause on our conversation for just a moment. You guys were looking at Kayla and I could tell you were really thinking about what she had to say. When we speak, we can help our listeners pay attention by trying to make eye contact with them, too. As you all are speaking, try glancing at everyone in the group, not just one person or me. Did you notice how I just looked at each one of you as I said that?<br><br>Now, who can try to glance at everyone as you add on to Kayla's idea about Allie wanting to be like the pro basketball players but people telling her she couldn't because she's a girl? |
| --- | --- |

This interaction touches on two challenges we notice in classroom discussions: listeners looking around or seemingly not paying attention to the speaker, and speakers directing a great majority of their comments to the teacher, even though they are supposed to be engaged in a *group* discussion. As soon as the conversation started, Ms. Davis reinforced the listening behavior with a positive presupposition that they were not only looking at Kayla as she spoke, but also thinking about what Kayla had to say. This reinforcement was followed by an explicit teaching point of how to connect with your "audience" while speaking to them. Ms. Davis continued with an invitation to have a go with what she had just taught. The whole interaction lasted just under a minute. Ms. Davis kept her language clear and concise and ended the exchange by linking back to Kayla's idea so that the teaching point didn't detract from meaning. In subsequent interactions, Ms. Davis might simply say, "Tell everyone" and break eye contact with the child. Or she might remind speakers to "look at the group" and nod to the group members. Becoming attentive listeners isn't something that typically happens overnight for children, but with opportunity and guidance, it will eventually become natural.

## Take Turns

One of the most foundational ground rules for oral communication that allows active participation to occur is taking turns. As adults, we seldom sit with our hands raised, waiting to be called upon by a facilitator to comment during a small-group discussion. Instead, we listen for a pause in the conversation, then start talking, lean in if we want to add something, and lift a finger or give another subtle sign to indicate we have something to say.

Knowing and using these social cues helps us monitor ourselves as well as others' participation. Again, young students still learning these cues may need them to be explicitly taught before internalizing them.

| MS. KELLEY | (*Discussing the level E book* Sad Monster) What are you thinking about the friends that Monster made? |
|---|---|
| JASMINE | (*Raises hand and waits to be called upon.*) |
| MS. KELLEY | You don't have to raise your hand. The others will listen, and when you're finished, they will share their thinking about the friends, too. Go ahead. |
| JASMINE | They were mean and wouldn't be his friend. |
| ERIC | Yeah, they were scared of him 'cause—'cause he's a monster. |
| JASMINE | But that one wasn't scared and played with him. |
| ERIC | It's like Marshall Armstrong (*referring to* Marshall Armstrong Is New to Our School *by David Mackintosh, 2011*). |
| MS. KELLEY | Say more about that. |
| ERIC | They didn't like Marshall Armstrong at first, but then they went to his house and saw he did cool stuff and then they liked him. |
| MS. KELLEY | He judged Marshall at first, but then gave him a chance and they became friends. How is that like *Sad Monster*? |
| JASMINE | That boy (*pointing to picture on the last page*) wasn't scared and played with Monster, and the other kids saw him playing with him and didn't get scared anymore. |
| MS. KELLEY | We haven't heard from Claudia yet. Who wants to invite Claudia into the conversation and ask her what she's thinking? |
| JASMINE | What do you think, Claudia? |
| CLAUDIA | He was just a little kid, but he wasn't scared. |
| ERIC | The other boy and girl was big. |
| CLAUDIA | Maybe he didn't know to be scared. |
| MS. KELLEY | I hadn't thought about that before. Wow, we learn so much when we all share our thinking together! |

In this excerpt, the teacher supports turn-taking with reminders and nudges. Later in the discussion, she notices that one student has not contributed to the conversation yet. Instead of directly asking Claudia, she nudges one of the students to ask her. Over time, with consistent interactions such as these, students will begin to figure out ways to enter the conversation and adopt the norm of noticing when someone hasn't had a chance to speak and inviting them into the conversation.

## Support Our Ideas with Evidence

When it comes to talking about books, being able to provide evidence from the text, our own experiences, or what we know about the world helps to clarify for others. This evidence often shows not only what the reader is thinking, but also how the reader came to his or her understanding.

| | |
|---|---|
| MR. PENN | (*Discussing the level A book* Mom Loves Hats) Which one do you think was her favorite hat? |
| CARMEN | The black one. |
| STELLA | The one with flowers. |
| MR. PENN | What makes you think the black one is her favorite and you think the flowered one is? |
| CARMEN | (*Turns to page with black hat.*) She's smiling. |
| STELLA | (*Turns to page with flowered hat.*) She's happy. |
| MR. PENN | (*To Stella*) How do you know? |
| STELLA | She's smiling so big (*gives a big smile to mimic the character's*). |
| MR. PENN | You girls are doing some important reading work. You're using the pictures to know how the character feels. Another way to know how she feels is to think about the words the author used. Let me show you what I mean. On this page it says, "Mom likes the purple hat" (*continues pointing out the "Mom likes" pattern on two more pages*). But look here, on the last page it says, "Mom *loves* the flowered hat." If she *likes* all the other hats but *loves* the flowered hat, it makes me think the flowered hat is probably her favorite. Did you see what I did? I used the words to help me think about what the character was thinking. You can do that too. Keep using the pictures to help you think about the story and use the words too. |

The work of reading and the work of discussing texts are very much intertwined in this example. They are all about thinking. Very often, the teaching we do to support talk routines will support students' use of reading strategies, and vice versa. Mr. Penn started by prompting students to support their thinking with evidence, and they responded with what they noticed in the pictures. The teacher then took advantage of this part of the discussion to reinforce how they supported their idea with evidence (talk goal), and then he taught the group another way to search for and use evidence in the text (reading strategy). Both will help students construct meaning and link back to the book to support their thinking as they discuss other books they read.

## Grow Ideas Together

Ryunosuke Satoro reminds us, "Individually we are one drop. Together, we are an ocean" (n.d.). As members of a learning community, it is our responsibility to both contribute to and grow from a collective body of knowledge and understanding with our peers. In conversations, we do this by growing ideas together—listening to and taking in the ideas of others, then adding to, negotiating, and sometimes respectfully disagreeing with what they say.

Listening with purpose is critical to growing ideas together. It helps us determine the main points another person is sharing, consider those points, and further explore them before moving on. This is very hard (even for adults). Sometimes we get distracted or our mind wanders. Sometimes we can't listen with purpose because we are so intent on sharing our idea. Over time, we learn to monitor ourselves within the conversation and attend to others so we can build ideas together. The following language is useful for growing ideas together:

- What are you thinking about what [student] said?

- Say more about that.

- Keep talking about that.

- Let's keep thinking about that together.

- Can someone add on to that idea?

- What else could we say about that?

- Do you all agree or disagree with what [student] just said? Why?

- What's another way to think about that idea?

- What are you wondering about that?

- Can someone take us to a place in the book that supports what [student] just said and say more about it to add to our thinking?

We've seen glimpses of this language throughout the examples we've looked at thus far. Let's look at another excerpt from a conversation where students are starting to naturally grow ideas together, with just a little prompting from the teacher, as they discuss the level J book *Our Clothes* (2001) by Jeni Wilson and Sue Davis:

| MS. SCOTT | What are you thinking about clothes now that you've read this book? |
|---|---|
| STEFANI | They help keep us safe. |
| MS. SCOTT | Say more about that. |
| STEFANI | We put our shoes on so our feet don't get hurt. |
| MAXWELL | And gloves and coats on to stay warm. |
| EVAN | If you didn't put on a hat and sunglasses and stuff when you play outside, then you'd get burnt up. |
| MS. SCOTT | So we know there are many ways clothes help to keep us safe. What else? |
| DESTINY | You wear them for different things. Like my mom always makes me wear a dress when we go to church to look nice. |
| MAXWELL | Yeah, and like for sports (*turning to page with photograph of a soccer game*) so you know who's on your team to pass the ball. |
| STEFANI | There's lots of ways clothes help. |

In the early parts of this excerpt, Maxwell and Evan stuck with the idea Stefani: contributed by providing more examples of how clothes keep them safe, one of the main ideas of the book. Destiny later connected her personal experiences of wearing specific clothes for certain occasions with a concept conveyed in the book. As the understandings of the book grew through conversation, Stefani was led to synthesize all that had been shared and determine one of the text's big ideas.

Our ultimate goal for readers is for them to consider the ideas in books. Collectively, when the basic yet essential conversation skills are in place, we reach this goal more efficiently, respectfully, and effectively. These are skills we all need, not only to be successful in discussing texts, but also to be successful in life.

# HATS TEACHERS MIGHT WEAR DURING TEXT DISCUSSIONS

Teachers take on many roles to support students with discussions (see Figure 7.4). At times we teach, explicitly modeling and demonstrating for students. At times we facilitate, setting up learning environments for students to work more independently and providing little nudges as needed. At times we join in the thinking and learning, engaging in reader-to-reader conversations. And at times we assess, sitting back as neutral observers, looking and listening for evidence of thinking. In a typical discussion, we seamlessly transition between multiple roles.

Figure 7.4
LEVELS OF SUPPORT

| Highest Support | | Lowest Support | |
|---|---|---|---|
| Teacher | Facilitator | Participant | Observer |
| explicit demonstration | furthering student thinking | equal contribution | gathering information for future instruction |

## Teacher Hat

We wear our teacher hat when we need to provide the highest levels of support, explicitly demonstrating what to attend to and how it leads to understanding. The focus for our instruction might support strategic actions that help construct understanding, or it may explicitly teach discussion behaviors or routines.

Scrimmaging in sports enables the coach to stop midplay, teach the players something (e.g., to notice which player is open), and start the game again, while encouraging players to try out what they've learned. This same thing happened when Ms. Davis "pushed pause" during the discussion about *Allie's Basketball Dream*. She gave the kids a specific way to attend to the speaker (eye contact) and coached them to use it.

Sometimes wearing our teacher hat means providing the language for kids to use. For example, when two students begin talking at the same time, a teacher could facilitate ("First Anthony, then Maeva"), or he or she could pause the conversation—stop the content talk—and teach a ground rule for conversation: "When two people start at the same time, look at each other and decide who will go first. Whoever goes first then invites the other person to talk: 'What were you going to say?' So, Anthony and Maeva, try it. Look at each other and decide who is going to go first." Explicitly supporting talk behaviors may mean providing the language for talk, prompting kids to try it out, or naming what kids did independently.

## Facilitator Hat

Our facilitator hat enables us to establish the procedures and conditions so the group can think and discuss together. Alternatively, we help students navigate the rules and routines for discussion.

Return to Mrs. Adams's conversation with her students about *Birds* and notice how she opened the conversation with a broad question: "So what's something you learned that was new or interesting to you?" As several students responded, Mrs. Adams followed up on Devin's comment of "They have different kinds of feathers" with more specific guidance: "Turn to page 5. What did you notice about . . . ?" As a facilitator, Mrs. Adams was listening for "doorways" in student comments to open and explore in depth. Consider this structure: lead with a broad, thought-provoking statement or question; listen for doorways and follow students' lines of thinking; and follow up with questions or comments that help students build ideas together.

Another attribute of effective facilitation is giving ample wait time. *Ample* means generous, liberal, sufficient. It's normal to find the silence that comes with waiting uncomfortable, but it's often what we need to gather our thoughts. Sometimes the most powerful contributions to conversations are made after a seemingly awkward moment of silence. So, the next time you give students something to think about and respond to and you begin to hear crickets chirping, restrain yourself from filling the silence too quickly. The time to think might be exactly what your students need.

## Participant Hat

We want students to be active and open in their thinking about texts, a goal that is met by talking with others. Having authentic conversations means sometimes joining the conversation as a fellow reader and talking *with* students, rather than trying to teach or facilitate. Students enjoy and learn from hearing our genuine excitement about books, wonderings about topics, and connections that help us understand what characters are going through. And as a bonus, it's fun for us as teachers, too!

## Observer Hat

Guided reading is an ideal venue to observe how students comprehend a text they have read. As we mentioned earlier in the chapter, talk helps make thinking visible, and the small-group setting allows for more voices to be heard. Wearing our observer hat allows us to witness the fruits of our labor and see how students apply what we taught.

It's important to note that wearing our observer hat isn't the same as wearing an evaluator's hat. Our focus isn't on determining whether students are right or wrong or making a judgment of whether they "got the book" or didn't. Instead, we listen for their ideas and questions and infer what they reveal about how students are thinking about text. We notice when they add on to another's idea, ask a follow-up question, or give a friend a chance to speak. We then build on the insights we glean from these observations when we introduce books and engage in conversations in the future.

The point of thinking about the hats we wear isn't for us to be able to name which hat we're wearing at a given time or spend a certain percentage of time wearing one hat or another. We want to gain an awareness of how our actions affect the dynamics of conversations and the level of support we provide for our students. Each has an important role in helping readers become proficient in talking about texts so that they can eventually do it without us.

As teachers of reading, we want all our students to be readers who think beyond the words on the page. Talking with others is one of the best tools teachers have to promote deep thinking. Discussions give kids opportunities to share joy and to explore ideas within books. The moments after kids read their guided reading books are precious. Those are the moments that bring us together. Our hope is that the talk after reading—the spontaneous reactions, debates about opinions, and excitement of new learning and connections—build theories in our students that reading is worthwhile and that each child's contribution is valued and brings meaning to this enjoyable experience.

# A Final Thought:
# TRUST

Our monthly work sessions to write this book frequently began by sharing what was on our minds about work and home. Often, one of us expressed a joy or trial of parenting, telling stories that related to a stage of child development (tantrums, fear of the dark, sleep habits, relating to others). We confided in one another about how we responded in certain situations—feeling proud of some, though we'd mishandled others—and we gave one another advice.

One afternoon, we discussed a recent insight of Kath's husband, Dan: "The good thing about parenting is that we have time—days, months, and years—to talk with the kids and help them grow up." As parents, we try our best and don't get things right every time. Sometimes we yell and wish we hadn't. Other times we're so busy rushing around that we neglect to truly listen to our kids to understand where they're coming from. We ask, *Am I present enough? Am I being too lenient or too strict? Am I teaching her the skills she needs to become a kind and caring person? Am I helping him become independent?* Parenting is a lifelong process. There is always tomorrow, the next day, and the day after that. Parenting is a series of opportunities to watch and listen and talk *with* our children about friendships and frustrations, fairness and injustices, good and bad, failing and persevering.

Teaching is similar to parenting in many of the same ways. We have good intentions to maximize every teachable moment. We care deeply about our students and want them all to succeed. Sometimes a lesson we plan for them hits the mark, and sometimes it falls short. In this quest for success we may doubt our actions and wonder: *Am I doing what's best? Am I scaffolding too much or too little? Am I seeing enough steady progress? Are my teaching points clear and concise? Are these texts too easy? Too hard? Are they interesting enough to engage my reluctant readers?* Not every opportunity will feel successful, even when we plan what we think is a dynamite lesson.

The good news for us is that teaching is a yearlong process. There is tomorrow, the next day, and the day after that. Like parenting, teaching permits us time with children. Maybe not as much time as we want, but time that is precious and valuable. Part of teaching means trusting that the many moments we have with our students over days and weeks throughout the school year matter.

Think of the student who walks into the classroom one morning and suddenly seems taller. You wonder if he's grown an inch overnight. Of course not! Reading growth is like that too. We may not notice every behavior our young readers are taking on or each vocabulary word they have learned, yet we know that growth is happening even when we don't see it day to day.

We trust the developmental process of students and remember that there are multiple ways to learn something. An unfamiliar phrase that initially confuses a student will eventually become a part of his lexicon. The child who speaks very little during small-group discussions will one day share her idea and the others will turn to her and listen. We develop relationships with students every day that build their trust in us and in themselves. We believe our many interactions empower students to take risks, learn from mistakes, wrestle with difficult problems, and share ideas. And through all this, we trust that they are learning in their own way, along the way.

We hope that reading this book has helped you gain trust in the decisions you make as a teacher. Trust that understanding a book for yourself first will allow you to expand your children's perspectives. Trust that a thoughtful introduction will guide your students to construct something meaningful and that you've set them up for a successful read. Trust that inviting students into a conversation after they finish reading will reveal important thinking. Trust that talking *with* them and following their lead during book conversations matters. Trust that if you miss the mark with one lesson, you've got it within you to closely watch, reflect, and refine for the next. Trust that when we lead with meaning, our children will develop into powerful readers who seek to understand every time they read.

# Appendix A

# DEVELOPING CRITERIA FOR TEXT SELECTION: TEXT CHARACTERISTICS THAT SUPPORT GROWTH

| **IF** I have evidence that suggests [students' interests, strengths, and needs based on their reading behaviors] . . . | **THEN** I'll select a book that [characteristics of texts that will offer opportunities to build on identified strengths and support identified needs]. |
|---|---|
| | |
| | |
| | |
| | |

## Appendix B

# GUIDED READING PLANNING SHEET

**Group/Students:** _____

**Date:** _____

**Running Record Student:** _____

**Running Record Book/Level:** _____

**New Book/Level:** _____

**Introducing the Text:**

*Meaning Statement:*


*Support (how book works, language structures, words):*


*Launch:*


**Anecdotal Notes:**

| Student: | Student: | Student: |
|---|---|---|
|  |  |  |
| Student: | Student: | Student: |
|  |  |  |

**Text Discussion:**


**Group Teaching Point:**


**Word Work:**

# REFERENCES

## Professional References

Allington, Richard, Kimberly McCuisten, and Monica Billen. 2015. "What Research Says About Text Complexity and Learning to Read." *The Reading Teacher* 68 (7): 491–501.

Barnhouse, Dorothy, and Vicki Vinton. 2012. *What Readers Really Do: Teaching the Process of Meaning Making*. Portsmouth, NH: Heinemann.

Beck, Isabel, Margaret McKeown, and Linda Kucan. 2002. *Bringing Words to Life*. New York: Guilford.

Cazden, Courtney. 2004. "The Value of Conversations for Language Development and Reading Comprehension." *Literacy Teaching and Learning* 9 (1): 5. http://files.eric.ed.gov/fulltext/EJ966158.pdf.

Clay, Marie. 1991. *Becoming Literate: The Construction of Inner Control*. Portsmouth, NH: Heinemann.

———. 1991. "Introducing a New Storybook to Young Readers (Impact Factor: 0.77)." *The Reading Teacher* 45 (4): 264–273. https://www.researchgate.net/journal/0034-0561_The_Reading_Teacher.

———. 1998. *By Different Paths to Common Outcomes*. Portland, ME: Stenhouse.

———. 2000. *Running Records for Classroom Teachers*. Portsmouth, NH: Heinemann.

———. 2001. *Change Over Time in Children's Literacy Development*. Portsmouth, NH: Heinemann.

———. 2005. *Literacy Lessons Designed for Individuals, Part One: Why? When? and How?* Portsmouth, NH: Heinemann.

————. 2013. *An Observation Survey of Early Literacy Achievement.* 3rd ed. Portsmouth, NH: Heinemann.

————. 2015. *Record of Oral Language: Observing Changes in the Acquisition of Language Structures.* New edition update.  Portsmouth, NH: Heinemann.

Cochran, Karen, and Bonnie Hain. 2012. *What Is Text Structure?* http://jplutt.weebly. com/uploads/5/7/1/6/57166409/what_is_text_structure.pdf.

Dutro, Susana, and Carrol Moran. 2003. "Rethinking English Language Instruction: An Architectural Approach." http://www.doe.in.gov/sites/default/files/curriculum/ rethinking-language-instruction.pdf.

Fay, Kathleen, and Suzanne Whaley. 2004. *Becoming One Community: Reading and Writing with English Language Learners.* Portland, ME: Stenhouse.

Fletcher, Ralph. 2013. *What a Writer Needs.* Portsmouth, NH: Heinemann.

Fountas, Irene C., and Gay Su Pinnell. 1998. *Word Matters: Teaching Phonics and Spelling in the Reading/Writing Classroom.* Portsmouth, NH: Heinemann.

————. 2006. *Teaching for Comprehending and Fluency: Thinking, Talking, and Writing About Reading, K–8.* Portsmouth, NH: Heinemann.

————. 2012. *Prompting Guide, Part 1 for Early Reading and Early Writing.* Portsmouth, NH: Heinemann.

————. 2017a. *The Fountas and Pinnell Literacy Continuum: A Tool for Assessment, Planning, and Teaching, Grades PreK–8.* Portsmouth, NH: Heinemann.

————. 2017b. *Guided Reading: Responsive Teaching Across the Grades.* Portsmouth, NH: Heinemann.

Goodman, Yetta. 1989. "Evaluation of Students." In *The Whole Language Evaluation Book,* ed. K. S. Goodman, Y. S. Goodman, and W. J. Hood. Portsmouth, NH: Heinemann.

Harrington, Janice. 2012. "Right Book, Right Time, Right Child.*" The New York Times.* http://www.nytimes.com/roomfordebate/2012/12/26/what-books-are-just-right-for-the-young-reader/right-book-right-time-right-child.

Jensen, Eric. n.d. "Principles of Brain-Based Learning." *Jensen Learning.* http://www. jensenlearning.com/principles.php.

Johnson, Pat. 2006. *One Child at a Time: Making the Most of Your Time with Struggling Readers, K–6.* Portland, ME: Stenhouse.

Johnson, Pat, and Katie Keier. 2010. *Catching Readers Before They Fall: Supporting Readers Who Struggle, K–4.* Portland, ME: Stenhouse.

Johnston, Peter. 2000. *Running Records: A Self-Tutoring Guide.* Portland, ME: Stenhouse.

Jones, Noel. 2013. "Widening the Lens: How Seeing and Understanding Develop Together." *Journal of Reading Recovery* 12 (2): 7.

King, Stephen. 2001. *On Writing: A Memoir of the Craft.* New York: Pocket Books.

Laminack, Lester, and Reba Wadsworth. 2015. *We ARE Readers: Flipping Reading Instruction into Writing Opportunities.* Portsmouth, NH: Heinemann.

Landrigan, Clare, and Tammy Mulligan. 2012. *Assessment in Perspective: Focusing on the Reader Behind the Numbers.* Portland, ME: Stenhouse.

Lindfors, Judith. 1999. *Children's Inquiry: Using Language to Make Sense of the World.* New York: Teachers College Press.

Lyons, Carol. 2003. *Teaching Struggling Readers: Using Brain-Based Research to Maximize Learning.* Portsmouth, NH: Heinemann.

McCullough, David. 2002. *John Adams.* New York: Touchstone.

Moll, Luis, Cathy Amanti, Deborah Neff, and Norma Gonzalez. 1992. "Funds of Knowledge." *Theory into Practice* 31 (2): 132–141.

National Public Radio. 2014. "Join *The Morning Edition Book Club*: We're Reading *Deep Down Dark*." NPR.org. http://www.npr.org/templates/transcript/transcript.php?storyId=369409338.

Nichols, Maria. 2006. *Comprehension Through Conversation: The Power of Purposeful Talk in the Reading Workshop.* Portsmouth, NH: Heinemann.

Parisi, Fabio, Pratyaksha Wirapati, and Felix Naef. 2007. "Identifying Synergistic Regulation Involving c-Myc and sp1 in Human Tissues." *Nucleic Acids Research* 35 (4). https://www.ncbi.nlm.nih.gov/pubmed/17264126.

Pinnell, Gay Su, and Irene C. Fountas. 1996. *Word Matters: Teaching Phonics and Spelling in the Reading/Writing Classroom.* Portsmouth, NH: Heinemann.

———. 2009. *When Readers Struggle: Teaching That Works.* Portsmouth, NH: Heinemann.

Randell, Beverly. 2000. *Shaping the PM Story Books.* Wellington, New Zealand: Gondwanaland.

Routman, Regie. 1996. *Literacy at the Crossroads: Critical Talk About Reading, Writing and Other Teaching Dilemmas.* Portsmouth, NH: Heinemann.

Satoro, Ryunosuke. n.d. BrainyQuote.com. http://www.brainyquote.com/quotes/quotes/r/ryunosukes167565.html.

Serravallo, Jennifer. 2014. *The Literacy Teacher's Playbook, Grades K–2.* Portsmouth, NH: Heinemann.

———. 2015. *The Reading Strategies Book: Your Everything Guide to Developing Skilled Readers.* Portsmouth, NH: Heinemann.

Szymusiak, Karen, Franki Sibberson, and Lisa Koch. 2008. *Beyond Leveled Books: Supporting Early and Transitional Readers in Grades K–5*. Portland, ME: Stenhouse.

Tobar, Hector. 2014. *Deep Down Dark: The Untold Stories of 33 Men Buried in a Chilean Mine, and the Miracle That Set Them Free*. New York: Farrar, Straus and Giroux.

Vygotsky, Lev. 1978. *Mind in Society: The Development of Higher Psychological Processes*. Boston: Harvard University Press.

WIDA. 2014. Board of Regents of the University of Wisconsin System, on behalf of WIDA—www.wida.us. Version 1.5, Revised 11/1/16. https://www.wida.us/get.aspx?id=540.

Zwiers, Jeff, and Marie Crawford. 2011. *Academic Conversations: Classroom Talk That Fosters Critical Thinking and Content Understandings*. Portland, ME: Stenhouse.

## Children's Works References

Barber, Barbara. 1996. *Allie's Basketball Dream*. New York: Scholastic.

Barrows, Annie. 2007. *Ivy and Bean Break the Fossil Record*. San Francisco: Chronicle.

Berger, Melvin, and Gilda Berger. 2006. *Dolphins and Porpoises*. New York: Scholastic.

Cherrington, Janelle. 2009. *The Yard Sale*. New York: Scholastic.

Cowley, Joy. 2005. *Chameleon!* New York: Scholastic.

Dahl, Roald. 1982. *The BFG*. New York: Farrar, Straus and Giroux.

Davies, Nicola. 2005. *Surprising Sharks*. Somerville, MA: Candlewick.

———. 2015. *I Don't Like Snakes*. Somerville, MA: Candlewick.

DiCamillo, Kate. 2006. *Mercy Watson Goes for a Ride*. Somerville, MA: Candlewick.

———. 2014. *Leroy Ninker Saddles Up*. Somerville, MA: Candlewick.

Dickey, Laurel. 1999. *Balloons*. Northampton, MA: Pioneer Valley.

Dufresne, Michele. 2000. *The Walk*. Northampton, MA: Pioneer Valley.

———. 2003. *Mom Loves Hats*. Northampton, MA: Pioneer Valley.

———. 2007. *At the Ocean*. Northampton, MA: Pioneer Valley.

———. 2013. *All About Ants*. Northampton, MA: Pioneer Valley.

———. 2014. *Jaxon's Animals*. Northampton, MA: Pioneer Valley.

———. 2015a. *Dogs or Cats?* Northampton, MA: Pioneer Valley.

———. 2015b. *Fireflies*. Northampton, MA: Pioneer Valley.

———. 2015c. *Where Does Your Pizza Come From?* Northampton, MA: Pioneer Valley.

Finnigan, Sean. 2006. *Baseball.* Northampton, MA: Pioneer Valley.

Fried, Mary. 1996. *The Farm*. Columbus: The Ohio State University.

Giles, Jenny. 2000. *Billy Can Count.* Barrington, IL: Rigby.

———. 2006. *Come On, Tim.* Austin, TX: Harcourt Achieve.

Harper, Lesley. 1992. *Carla's Ribbons*. Rocky River, OH: Kaeden.

Henkes, Kevin. 1991. *Chrysanthemum*. New York: HarperCollins.

Hutchins, Pat. 1983. *You'll Soon Grown into Them, Titch.* New York: Greenwillow.

Jenkins, Steve, and Robin Page. 2003. *What Do You Do with a Tail Like This?* Boston: Houghton Mifflin.

Kline, Suzy. 2006. *Horrible Harry and the Triple Revenge*. New York: Penguin.

Lawrence, Trina. 2015. *Garbage to Garden.* Northampton, MA: Pioneer Valley.

Lewis, Rose. 2012. *Birds.* Northampton, MA: Pioneer Valley.

Lovell, Scarlett, and Diane Snowball. 1995. *Is This a Monster?* Greenvale, NY: Mondo Educational Publishing.

Mackintosh, David. 2011. *Marshall Armstrong Is New to Our School.* New York: Harry N. Abrams.

Martin Jr., Bill, and Eric Carle. 1996. *Brown Bear, Brown Bear, What Do You See?* New York: Henry Holt.

McDonald, Megan. 2006. *Stink and the Incredible Super-Galactic Jawbreaker*. Somerville, MA: Candlewick.

———. 2013. *Stink and the World's Worst Super-Stinky Sneakers*. Somerville, MA: Candlewick.

Oxenbury, Helen, and Michael Rosen. 1997. *We're Going on a Bear Hunt*. New York: Simon and Schuster.

Price, Hugh. 1997. *In the Days of the Dinosaurs: Pterosaur's Long Flight*. Barrington, IL: Rigby.

Randell, Beverley. 1994. *Mushrooms for Dinner.* Barrington, IL: Rigby.

———. 1996. *Blackberries.* Barrington, IL: Rigby.

———. 1996. *The Hungry Kitten.* Barrington, IL: Rigby.

———. 1997. *Rescuing Nelson.* Barrington, IL: Rigby.

———. 1998. *Pigs.* Barrington, IL: Rigby.

———. 2006. *Father Bear Goes Fishing.* Austin, TX: Harcourt.

Renton, Will. 2014. *Cat Naps with Oliver.* Northampton, MA: Pioneer Valley.

Rossetti-Shustak, Bernadette. 2005. *I Love You Through and Through.* New York: Scholastic.

Russell-Arnot, Elizabeth. 1999. *Bats.* Austin, TX: Harcourt Brace Jovanovich.

Rylant, Cynthia. 1987. *Henry and Mudge: The First Book.* New York: Scholastic.

———. 1988. *Henry and Mudge and the Sparkle Days*. New York: Scholastic.

———. 1996. *Henry and Mudge in Puddle Trouble.* New York: Simon and Schuster.

———. 1997. *Poppleton.* New York: Scholastic.

Sanders, Jay. 2004. *Misa Learns to Ride.* Barrington, IL: Rigby.

Smith, Annette. 2000a. *Bedtime.* Barrington, IL: Rigby.

———. 2000b. *New Boots.* Barrington, IL: Rigby.

———. 2001. *Kitty Cat and the Paint.* Barrington, IL: Rigby.

Smith, Annette, Jenny Giles, and Beverley Randell. 2000. *The Toy Box.* Barrington, IL: Rigby.

Staman, Ann. 2002. *Sad Monster.* Benton Harbor, MI: Educators Publishing Service.

———. 2008. *The Fox Who Cried "Help!"* Ottawa, ON: Educators Publishing Service.

Stewart, Melissa. 2011. *Frog or Toad? How Do You Know?* Berkley Heights, NJ: Enslow.

———. Which Animal Is Which? series. New York: Enslow.

Thaler, Mike. 1994. *The Gym Teacher from the Black Lagoon.* New York: Scholastic.

Wild, Margaret. 2006. *Fox.* La Jolla, CA: Kane/Miller.

Willems, Mo. 2013. *I'm a Frog!* New York: Disney-Hyperion.

Wilson, Jeni, and Sue Davis. 2001. *Our Clothes.* Barrington, IL: Rigby.

Wood, Audrey, and Don Wood. 1987. *Heckedy Peg*. New York: Harcourt Brace Jovanovich.

Woolley, Marilyn. 2009. *Big Ships Need Tugboats.* Temekula, CA: Okapi Educational Publishing.

Yates, Vicki. 2008. *Travel: Then and Now.* Chicago: Heinemann Library.

# INDEX